PRACTICAL
WOODLAND
STALKING

For George

PRACTICAL
WOODLAND
STALKING

GRAHAM DOWNING

Acknowledgements

All photography by Graham Downing except
Lloyd French, p108, p110
Jackson Rifles, p34
David Mason, p9, p23
Matthew Peaster, p3, p15, p47, p77, p88, p101, p102, p112
Brent Stapelkamp/BDS, p48
Charles Smith-Jones, p97
The Deer Initiative, p53, p178

Thanks to Dr Arnold Cooke and Ray Tabor for use of their protocol for assessing deer activity and damage.

First published in the UK in 2010
by Quiller, an imprint of Quiller Publishing Ltd

British Library Cataloguing-in-Publication Data
A catalogue record for this book
is available from the British Library

ISBN 978 1 84689 075 8

Printed in Malta
Book and jacket design by Sharyn Troughton

Quiller

An imprint of Quiller Publishing Ltd
Wykey House, Wykey, Shrewsbury, SY4 1JA
Tel: 01939 261616 Fax: 01939 261606
E-mail: info@quillerbooks.com
Website: www.countrybooksdirect.com

Contents

Introduction

EARLY IN THE MORNING one cold, late December day, crystals of frost glinted in the headlights of my car as I drew into the meadow beside the deserted farmyard and turned off the engine. Outside, the frozen ground was hard beneath my feet and the icy breath of winter glanced against my face as I turned my head towards the south-eastern horizon and searched for the first grey fingers of dawn.

Weather forecasts had been checked and rechecked the previous evening and a provisional plan made for my morning stalk, but now the wind direction was confirmed. I had tested it just a few minutes previously, pulling into a lay-by on the hilltop over which I had come just half a mile before reaching the farm. On the higher ground the cold breeze swept uninterrupted across the open fields of the old wartime aerodrome and by standing outside the car on the quiet country road, I had been able to determine its true direction. Orientating the photocopied map which lay beside me on the passenger seat, I could now finalise the details of my morning mission.

On the far side of a field of winter wheat I could just see the outline of a thick, ancient hedgerow with its centuries-old rampart and ditch which marked the parish boundary, and beyond it the dark bulk of a wood. I had studied both of them in detail on the map, of course, and knew their directions and dimensions. I had assessed their juxtaposition with the other nearby woods and game crops and checked the gently undulating contours of the adjacent fields. But that had been in theory; this was for real.

Only once before had I visited the farm. It was a fortnight previously that the farmer had driven me around the property in his pick-up to show me the general lie of the land and we had discussed his need to manage the deer population. Evidence of deer had been everywhere –

well-used fallow paths leading in and out of the woods, muntjac tracks along the field edges and, most significantly, damage to the young trees which had been planted under a farm woodland scheme. Saplings had been stripped and their crowns nipped out by fallow deer, while the tree guards that had been supposed to protect the young trees had been comprehensively trashed. At one point as we had driven together down a narrow track, a muntjac buck had darted across in front of the vehicle. Something needed to be done to reduce the deer damage: would I be prepared to help?

Two weeks and several telephone conversations later, here I was, a photocopy of a formal stalking agreement in the inside zip pocket of my stalking jacket alongside my firearm certificate, a pair of binoculars around my neck, a rifle on my shoulder and the expectations of landowner, farmer and gamekeeper weighing heavily upon me. For ten years I had been stalking deer, firstly under the supervision of professional guides and then with one or other of my friends on their own ground. I had regularly hunted red and roe deer in Scotland and had devoted long days in late winter to stalking roe does and muntjac in the East Anglian breckland, but this was the first time that I had stepped out onto a stalking beat for which I was solely responsible. There would be nobody to guide me, nobody to make useful suggestions or offer local knowledge, nobody to blame when things went wrong. I was finally flying solo. The words my old driving instructor had uttered on the afternoon when I passed my test came back to me: 'Congratulations, this is where you start learning'.

That stalking trip was many years ago, but I remember it well, for it is recorded in detail in my diary. The careful stalk along that ancient hedge, the entry into the wood at first light and the muntjac which I carelessly 'bumped' as I picked my way down a ride, deeply rutted by the wheel-tracks of the gamekeeper's Land Rover. Then there was the fallow pricket which I spotted eighty yards ahead of me in the wood, fraying his antlers against an ash tree. He never heard the shot which killed him.

And then there were the two roe does, an adult and her yearling youngster, which I had seen in a game crop. I had been convinced when I spotted those two pairs of ears sticking above the gently fluttering tops of the straw-coloured maize leaves that they belonged to fallow deer, because the farmer had told me quite definitely that there were no roe on the property. But as I watched them slowly exit the maize and wander in the grey morning light towards a nearby wood, then tuck themselves down beneath a hedge, their real identity became evident.

● Roe deer in winter

I had belly-crawled on the frozen ground along the edge of the game crop and stalked down into a hollow in order to get a safe shot at those two roe. The first had fallen where it stood; the second had bolted through the hedgerow and collapsed just thirty yards out into the next field. I remember the look of approval from the farmer as his pick-up arrived while I was loading the three carcasses into my vehicle, and his surprise at seeing the two roe. It had been a good outing, my position was quickly secured and I still stalk that same ground today.

But the words of that driving instructor were so right. You can learn a huge amount when stalking alongside a professional guide or accompanying your friends, either whilst out hunting in the field or talking afterwards together in the pub. Likewise four days spent on a DSC 1 course will never be time wasted, because whatever your level of experience, you will always learn from the instructors and the other course participants alike. But the real learning starts when you have to make the decisions for yourself.

It is at that point when conventional techniques, equipment and accessories are put to the test and accepted, rejected or modified to meet both the requirements of the ground over which you stalk and the characteristics of your individual hunting style and philosophy. In the following pages I have set down some of the conclusions which I have reached about woodland stalking, about equipment, techniques and management practices. They are my own views and they are not definitive, because I am still learning: when you are dealing with wild animals and wild places, that learning process never stops.

Graham Downing
Chediston 2010

PART 1
GETTING STARTED

1

A Question of Calibre

GATHER HALF A DOZEN DEER STALKERS in the same room and there will always be at least one thing that they will argue about. The choice of rifles and ammunition for deer stalking is an intensely personal matter and one about which there is always room for lively, and sometimes heated, debate.

Such debate was reignited within the deer stalking world in 2005 when the UK Government first announced its intention to permit the use of certain .22 centre fire calibres for the shooting of the smaller deer species in England. The suggestion divided deer stalking opinion into two camps. On one side stood those who used .22 centre fire rifles for the control of foxes and who welcomed the prospect of using the same firearms for shooting muntjac, Chinese water deer and possibly even roe. They were supported by those who saw the move as a small but significant liberalisation which placed more choice back into the hands of the shooter. However, the proposed change was not greeted with unalloyed enthusiasm by other deer stalkers, who voiced their concerns that a switch from a larger to a smaller bullet would have an adverse effect upon welfare. In short, that it would lead to more wounded deer.

When Parliament finally approved the amendment to the 1991 Deer Act more than two years later in October 2007, the use of .22 centre fire rifles firing a 50 grain bullet producing 1,000 foot pounds of muzzle energy was approved for muntjac and Chinese water deer, but not for roe. The debate within the world of deer and deer management had done two things. Firstly, it had redrawn the legal baseline for the choice of firearms for deer stalking in England and Wales, but secondly it had also restated the essential truth that selection of a firearm for the hunting of any quarry must be matched to the animal's size, strength and body weight.

When a bullet strikes a large animal such as a deer, it first of all has to punch through the skin and enter the body cavity. As it does so it expands, disrupting and destroying any vital organs it finds in its path, before exiting the body. The bullet also delivers a knock-down blow to its target and, crudely speaking, the larger and heavier the bullet, the more punch it packs. The 'stopping power' of a bullet is very important, and an essential factor in its ability to put an animal on the ground and keep it there, so that the stalker is not obliged to set off on a long hunt in pursuit of a wounded – albeit perhaps mortally wounded – deer. Whilst it is quite true that a small, fast, flat-shooting bullet, delivered with surgical precision to the vital organs, will kill a large animal, that animal may travel a long way before collapsing, and that is assuming the stalker's aim was good. None of us is a perfect shot, and we delude ourselves if we think we are, so the stalker's bullet must have sufficient energy to effect a clean kill even if it does not strike exactly where the shooter intended it to. There must be at least some margin for error.

Any sensible shooter will do his best to match his firepower against the quarry which he intends to hunt, and this is as true for the shotgunner as it is for the rifleman. When he goes goose shooting, a wildfowler normally carries in his pocket or cartridge belt a suitable quantity of high velocity, heavy load cartridges containing large sized shot. He might even take with him a large calibre shotgun such as a 10 bore to fire them from. In just the same way, the hedgerow rabbit hunter eschews the .177 air rifle in favour of the .22, and the fox shooter prefers the .22 centre fire rifle to its rimfire cousin. He knows that, at short range, a .22 rimfire when used accurately will kill a fox, but that the centre fire gun can deliver far more power with great accuracy over much longer distances.

Exactly the same decision is made by those who travel overseas to shoot large game. I well recall seeing a very good friend shoot at an extremely large moose in the Lithuanian forest with his .270. The animal had been disturbed by the beaters on a driven boar hunt and was trotting slowly through an area of open brush. My friend, a very experienced rifleman, fired first at the animal's chest, but was surprised to see the moose shrug off the shot as if nothing had happened. His second and third shots were likewise directed at the heart and lung area, but still the animal didn't flinch. In desperation, thinking that his riflescope had been knocked out of zero and his shots had gone awry, he sighted along the barrel and fired at the neck. The animal dropped on the spot. However, when the head forester gralloched and

● The muntjac may be the smallest of the British deer species, but this tough little animal can nevertheless be hard to stop

dismembered the beast, the first three bullets were all found to have entered the chest, perfectly on target. They simply had insufficient knock-down power to drop such a large animal quickly.

Wounded muntjac do not have the huge body mass of an adult moose. But they do run away and they may be extremely hard to find, even if the wound eventually proves fatal. Of course every deer stalker ought to be sufficiently competent to be able to place his bullet accurately into the target area, and around 13,000 have demonstrated their marksmanship by passing the shooting test necessary to obtain a stalking qualification. But shooting at targets on the range and at deer in the wood are two very different things indeed, and bullets do not always go where they were intended.

So where does this leave the deer stalker who is pondering the apparently bewildering variety of calibres available to him?

● Around 13,000 stalkers have demonstrated their marksmanship by passing the shooting test necessary to obtain a stalking qualification

The considered choice of others is always a good starting point. In 2003 the British Association for Shooting and Conservation (BASC) conducted a survey of its deer stalking members which revealed that the three most popular calibres were .243, .270 and .308, a result which closely matches a survey of British Deer Society (BDS) members conducted in the same year. BASC additionally asked its members which species they shot with their rifles, at which point it became clear that for shooting muntjac, Chinese water deer and roe, the .243 was by far the most popular calibre, though for red, fallow and sika, both the .270 and .308 scored highly.

For years I have used a 150 grain .308 bullet for shooting all British deer species. Rated at around 2,700 foot pounds muzzle energy, it delivers sufficient stopping power to put down any deer which the UK stalker is likely to encounter, up to and including the largest woodland red stag, while I have also used it to great effect on driven wild boar. There can be no doubt that, for UK quarry species, this round has the ability to put an animal on the ground and keep it there, and let us remember that the objective of the deer stalker is to kill a deer and to find it afterwards, preferably without a long and nerve-wracking follow-up. The .308, the sporting version of the highly successful 7.62 x 51 military cartridge, is also a comfortable round to shoot; one which does not produce excessive recoil even when fired from a relatively lightly built sporting rifle. If there is one disadvantage to the .308, then it is the pronounced drop which this round has at longer distances, which means that the stalker must put in sufficient practice on the range to ensure that he knows exactly how much elevation to compensate for when shooting at more distant quarry.

It is to avoid this bullet drop that some stalkers prefer the .270, which with its higher velocity offers a flatter trajectory and therefore less need for downrange compensation. The .270 provides bags of knock-down energy but also has a slightly unfortunate reputation for being noisy and heavy on the shoulder, though the noise and to some extent the recoil can be corrected by the use of a sound moderator.

For those who stalk only the smaller UK species of deer, the .243 really provides all the answers. Rated at around 2,000 foot pounds of

● For shooting roe bucks and muntjac during the summer, when no larger species is in season, the .243 Win is a perfect choice

● This 9.3 mm over-and-under double rifle offers a rapid second shot, which is particularly useful when hunting large driven game such as wild boar. Note the low powered Schmidt & Bender riflescope to assist with rapid target acquisition

● The 9.3 x 74 cartridge packs a heavy punch for moose or wild boar

● The .300 Winchester Magnum is suitable for hunting soft skinned African plains game

muzzle energy and 3,000 feet per second with a 100 grain bullet, it is fast, flat shooting and extremely comfortable on the shoulder, the lack of recoil making it particularly easy to see the reaction of a shot deer through the riflescope. If I were to shoot nothing but roe or muntjac, then this is the cartridge which I would select for year-round use, though in my experience the 100 grain .243 bullet does not have the stopping power of the 150 grain .308 or .270. As it is, I tend to pick up my .243 as soon as the fallow buck season closes on 1 May. For summer shooting of muntjac and roe bucks, when no larger species features on the menu, then it is ideal.

There are two factors that signal the need for a larger round with more stopping power: body mass and adrenaline. When shooting at large game such as wild boar, moose or, in Africa, the larger antelope species, then additional downrange energy is called for, and two popular cartridges which are equally at home in the Scandinavian forest or the bushveldt, are the .300 Win Mag and the 9.3 x 74. The former is faster and flatter shooting, which is of particular benefit when hunting African plains game, at which it is often necessary to take a rather longer range shot than would be usual in the UK. The latter, with its range of heavy bullet weights, packs a formidable punch, though still not such a devastating blow as that classic African cartridge, the .375 Holland & Holland.

● Under most circumstances the UK stalker will hope to take his shot at an animal which is stationary and totally unaware of his presence

Under most circumstances the UK stalker will hope to take his shot at an animal which is stationary and totally unaware of the hunter's presence. In this situation a deer which is correctly struck through the chest or neck with an appropriately sized bullet will usually drop close to where it was standing when the shot was taken. Chest shot animals may run, but they will not usually run far, and they should be relatively easy to find.

But things may well be different if the quarry is aware of the imminent danger it faces from a human predator. When a prey animal such as a deer is alerted to imminent danger, adrenaline is released into the body, giving it additional reserves of energy with which to flee and to fight against the disability caused by a major wound. Thus while an animal that is unaware of the hunter's presence will usually drop nearby when correctly shot, one that has winded, seen or heard the predator that is pursuing it may have the capability of running much further and can thus be much more difficult to find, even if it is stone dead when it is finally discovered. This fact is of particular significance when hunting driven quarry such as wild boar or moose, which is why those who hunt driven boar or running moose regularly look for a cartridge which has additional reserves of stopping power such as the .300 Win Mag or the 9.3 mm, both of which are favoured by

● A welcome sight to any stalker: no need for any nerve-wracking follow-up with this muntjac doe

experienced moose hunters in Sweden. It is also the reason why, having taken an apparently good shot at an unsuspecting target, it is a good idea to wait for a few minutes before going to look for it. There is no sense in prompting the apparently dying animal to summon up sufficient strength to get to its feet once more and flee from the approaching human.

● A Swedish moose hunter with his .300 Winchester Magnum

There are, therefore, many advantages to be gained from selecting the larger calibre in preference to the smaller one, especially when a variety of different species may be encountered on a particular stalking trip. But what are the disadvantages? One of them, clearly, is recoil, and most shooters of average build would probably find repetitive use of anything larger than a .308 or .30-06, for example when practising on a range, to be uncomfortable. Another is carcass damage; there is no doubt that a large bullet can make quite a mess of a roe or muntjac carcass if by misfortune it goes through shoulders or loins. But then, so can a 100 grain bullet from a .243. If a bullet of whatever size is correctly placed in the target area of the chest, then carcass damage should not be an issue, but if it is not, then no matter how dainty the round, you can expect a bit of extra work with the butcher's knife when you come to dress out the carcass yourself, or some sucking of teeth, shaking of heads and financial deductions if you propose to deliver it to the game dealer.

● A big red forest stag pumped up with testosterone in the rut is the largest deer the UK stalker will have to deal with

● The law in England and Wales permits the use of certain .22 centre fire cartridges for the killing of muntjac

Consideration must also be given to bullet design. The law requires the use of expanding ammunition for shooting deer, but bullet construction may allow differently designed projectiles to expand in different ways and at different rates. While the vermin shooter may require rapid expansion of his fast-travelling round in order to dispatch small, thin-skinned animals, the deer stalker needs a more solidly constructed bullet which will expand more slowly, delivering most of its energy into the animal before exiting in order to ensure a visible blood trail. Waiting on the horizon is the debate about whether in future deer stalkers may be obliged, as many shotgunners already are, to dispense with lead projectiles and switch to non-toxic alternatives. The issues of lead deposition in the environment and lead bullet fragments in game meat are already live in some countries and a switch away from lead to, for example, solid copper bullets could affect terminal ballistics and potentially have a significant impact upon deer welfare.

As for the .22 centre fire calibres with which this discussion started, there can be no doubt that in experienced hands they are excellent for smaller quarry. However, so far as deer stalking is concerned, unless you are proposing to shoot only muntjac and Chinese water deer in England and Wales or roe in Scotland, they will be of no use to you.

2 Sight and Sound

A MODERN, newly manufactured stalking rifle is a precision instrument, but it can only be as accurate as the sight with which it is fitted allows it to be. There is little point in purchasing the perfect sporting firearm and marrying it with a second rate riflescope which will fail to deliver utterly reliable accuracy, time after time, irrespective of the rigours of everyday handling.

Like most other accessories to be found in the shooting field, riflescopes are manufactured to a wide range of different standards, determined largely by cost of manufacture. At the budget end of the spectrum are some very sound products, made in the Far East, which are absolutely ideal for air rifles and light rimfire calibres. Most, however, are entirely unsuitable for a stalking rifle which requires a riflescope that will maintain a rock solid zero despite round after round of punishing recoil from a heavy cartridge.

The products that come from the reputable manufacturers at the top end of the market really are in a different league. The materials which they are built from, the tolerances to which they are manufactured, the coatings which are applied to their precision optics to ensure optimum light transmission; all these things contribute to the excellence of their overall quality, while you can be assured that a riflescope from a top-drawer European or US manufacturer has been tested to exacting standards. In designing and developing their new products such companies employ a fiendish range of devices which are used to torture optical equipment until it screams for mercy. Lenses are deliberately scuffed and abraded, water is forced into instrument casings and riflescopes are subjected to temperature fluctuations from -20 to +55°C, all in the interests of ensuring quality. Meanwhile an inertia machine replicates the recoil to which a riflescope is subjected when a rifle is

● A riflescope from a top-drawer European manufacturer, such as this Swarovski Z6, can be guaranteed to perform with consistent reliability over many years of hard service

fired, a new model being subjected to thousands of 'rounds' in order to ensure the stability of the reticle.

Products from top drawer manufacturers with reputations to protect will also carry a lifetime guarantee, so that in the unlikely event that anything does go wrong, you can get the riflescope fixed or replaced, even years after buying it. The serious deer stalker who uses such an instrument in the field can be absolutely confident that it will perform consistently and with complete reliability under the toughest of conditions. Confidence in one's equipment plays a huge part in success at any form of shooting and for this reason if for no other, the old advice that you should spend as much again on your riflescope as you do on your rifle makes a great deal of sense.

But not everyone need dismiss the middle market manufacturers. There are plenty of keen stalkers who, for one reason or another, will go stalking no more than half a dozen times a year or even less, perhaps firing only four or five rounds at live quarry in the course of a season and maybe ten times that number on the range. Whether someone who falls into that category really needs a scope that is designed for total reliability during repeated use under punishing conditions is open to question.

For the woodland stalker there are, however, a few general considerations regarding riflescopes which should be particularly borne in mind, whichever price bracket he is exploring. Firstly there is the matter of magnification. The higher the magnification, the more

● For the woodland stalker who takes most of his shots at close range, a relatively low powered fixed magnification riflescope is ideal

restricted is the field of view. While some degree of magnification is important, too much can be a positive disadvantage. For the low ground stalker who will probably take most of his shots at relatively short range, often in woodland, it is better to have relatively low magnification and a wider field of view which assists rapid target acquisition. Magnification which is too high actually makes more difficult the process of picking up a target in the scope when the rifle is raised to the shoulder, and a scope which is too powerful may mean that the shooter has to search against a difficult backdrop of foliage for the target which he has spotted and identified with his binoculars. Even if this search takes only a fraction of a second, it could mean the difference between a successful shot and failure with a nervous, twitchy animal which senses that there is danger nearby.

A variable power scope is increasingly the choice of the deer stalker today, but even when selecting a variable scope, it is important to choose the instrument which will do what you want it to. For the woodland stalker that means operating at around 6x magnification, which enables him to pick up a target the moment the rifle is mounted. Much more than that can start to put the hunter at a disadvantage when taking shots at close range in woodland. Where longer range shooting over more open ground is involved, then 8x or 10x magnification may be advantageous, while the dedicated safari hunters shooting plains game over long distances will opt for even more magnification.

● This Aimpoint 'red dot' sight, here mounted on a combination rifle/shotgun, is designed for hunting driven quarry and does not magnify the target

Conversely, the hunter who is planning to try his hand overseas at driven game such as wild boar is well advised to look for magnification of 1.5x or 2x. Many serious driven game hunters now dispense with the riflescope altogether in favour of a 'red dot' sight with little or no magnification whatsoever. I have used these sights when hunting overseas and found them very accurate and easy to use.

For a device which was first introduced commercially as early as 1904, the riflescope has seen some remarkable developments in recent years, some of which are highly relevant to the woodland stalker operating at relatively short ranges and some of which are of less significance. Falling into the latter category are bullet-drop compensating turrets, which enable the shooter to adjust his point of aim to compensate for the elevation required when shooting over longer distances. An elevating turret has on it a distance scale which is graduated using known ballistic data relating to the ammunition which is being used. When the shooter clicks the turret to the known range of the target, the scope compensates for the exact drop of the bullet at the selected range. Some manufacturers, such as Zeiss, customise their turrets with a calibrated strip which matches the ballistic data of the ammunition that is being used. Others, like Leupold, offer a precision laser-engraved custom dial. However, effective use of bullet drop compensation technology requires accurate calculation of range, which in turn ideally requires the use of a further bit of technology in the form of a laser range-finder. Inevitably, though, Zeiss offer a hunting scope

● Effective use of bullet-drop compensation technology requires accurate range calculation, for which this Leica laser range finder is a useful tool

with bullet drop compensation and its own built-in laser range finder, in which the range to the target is shown in the scope's display. It is an awesome piece of kit, which is priced accordingly.

While technology of this sort, derived inevitably from the field of military sniping, may be applicable to the hunter shooting at long range in wide open spaces, it is less appropriate to the low ground stalker in Britain, who will more often be called upon to take his shot at close range and at only a moment's notice in which there may be sufficient time available only to point and shoot. Some deer stalkers genuinely enjoy using technology. I know quite a few of them, and some are really excellent hunters whose love of gadgets is coupled with a genuine understanding of the wild animals they pursue. My personal hunting philosophy, however, is to keep things simple, for I believe we can easily become over-reliant on technology in hunting, just as we already are in so many other aspects of modern living. We humans have been hunting animals successfully for hundreds of thousands of years with the most basic technology and we are quite capable of doing so today. My preference, therefore, is to use relatively simple equipment with which I am absolutely familiar, to allow instinct to take over and to enable my own brain to make whatever adjustments may be required. It usually works.

One relatively recent development in riflescope technology which is of great benefit to the woodland stalker, however, is the illuminated

● The Zeiss V69, which offers either an illuminated dot or an illuminated cross in one reticle, clearly demonstrates the value of having an illuminated reticle when hunting in low light conditions

reticle. This electronic gadget enables the stalker to light up the aiming point of the reticle to make it more easily visible in low light. There is a wide variety of designs, with some manufacturers using an illuminated dot, others a cross or even a more complex grid of circles, holdover bars and windage marks. The intensity of the illumination may be altered, perhaps by turning a rotating turret, as with Schmidt & Bender or by repeatedly pressing a button, as with Docter, while some manufacturers such as Swarovski even offer pre-set illumination levels which enable you to select a preferred setting. Essentially, though, you should have the scope set to a low intensity illumination in the lowest light conditions, for example at the start of an early morning stalk, and increase the intensity setting as daylight improves. The human eye is very sensitive to light, and you should avoid having the aiming point too bright in relation to the overall image which you see through the eyepiece. When the light level reaches that of full daylight, then turn the illuminated reticle off altogether unless you have a daylight setting. Retro-fitting both of illuminated reticles and bullet-drop compensating turrets is possible with some of the top-end riflescopes.

An illuminated reticle is a real boon when shooting in those first few minutes at dawn or late in the evening, especially under dense woodland canopies, for it enables you to pick up the correct point of aim instantly, without any guesswork, and to shoot quickly and instinctively. However, if your illuminated reticle does not have an automatic time-out off switch, then do remember to turn it off manually when you put your rifle away, because otherwise the battery will run down very quickly. When you next come to need it, probably in the middle of a wood very early in the morning with a deer temptingly silhouetted sixty yards away in the near-darkness, it will not work.

Sound moderators

Take any group of middle aged shooters, put them around a dinner table in a busy restaurant or in the bar of a crowded pub, raise the noise level by adding some background music, and a fair proportion of them will almost certainly be unable to hear what is being said to them. Noise-induced deafness is the inevitable consequence of repeated exposure to gunshot noise, whether from shotgun or rifle; it is commonplace, it is debilitating and it is extremely irksome both to the sufferer and to those who seek to communicate with him. Ask my wife.

Nobody shoots on a range without hearing protection, but how many riflemen use earplugs, let alone headphone-type hearing protection, whilst deer stalking? Very few, I would suggest. The nature of stalking requires the hunter to make full use of all his senses and without the ability to hear low volume sounds such as birdsong – whether it be the 'all is OK' sound of a spring woodland at dawn or the warning call of a blackbird which signals that your presence has been noted and that you had better take more care – then the stalker's hunting ability is compromised. If he cannot hear the pigeons clappering from an ivy-covered oak, the distant bark of a muntjac or the gentle crunch of boots on dead leaves, then he is at a disadvantage.

Not often do I concede that our addiction to over-officious, nanny-state health and safety legislation provides anything that is good or worthwhile, but in the field of deer stalking it has, I accept, produced at least one benefit: the sound moderator.

Only a few years ago the sound moderator, or 'silencer' as it was then called, was something more usually associated with the world of the political assassin or with James Bond. 'Silencers' were employed by people in films who carried rifles around in briefcases which they could assemble in seconds and then use – perfectly zeroed of course – to dispatch their victims at inordinate range before slipping away unnoticed. The idea of the police allowing the ordinary deer stalker to possess such an object of infamy was utterly preposterous. To seek a 'silencer' for your deer rifle was to suggest that dark deeds were being planned. At best, poaching. At worst, something quite unspeakable.

Enter the health and safety officer. If shooters were not permitted by their firearms licensing departments to reduce the very loud bang emitted by their rifles, and their hearing was in consequence impaired, then would not the police be responsible? Moreover, could the police not be sued by deaf rifle shooters? Good point, agreed the Forensic Science Service, and very quickly the prejudice against sound

 Today almost all professional stalkers and a large and growing number of recreational stalkers use sound moderators

moderators evaporated. Nowadays almost all professional stalkers and a large and growing number of recreational stalkers use sound moderators.

This simple piece of kit does not of course silence a rifle. Nothing can actually eliminate the audible noise emitted by such a weapon when it detonates a centre fire cartridge. It does, however, reduce the volume by 20 dB or more. Indeed, some manufacturers claim up to 30 dB noise reduction. In practical terms a .243, when fitted with the popular Reflex T8 sound moderator, sounds about the same as a .410 shotgun firing a short-cased cartridge.

Not surprisingly, this offers the deer stalker very considerable benefits indeed. Apart from the advantages to one's own hearing, it greatly reduces the disturbance caused to residents when shooting close to farmsteads and houses early in the morning or late in the evening. Equally importantly, it reduces the disturbance caused to the deer themselves. Whereas the deafening report of an unmoderated rifle may send a herd high-tailing it into the next county, the sound of a shot

● The popular Reflex T8 sound moderator sleeved over the barrel of a .243 Mannlicher rifle.

from a rifle fitted with a moderator will often cause little or no alarm, thus enabling the stalker to take a second or subsequent shot if he wishes to do so.

I was reminded of this whilst stalking stags in Scotland with my wife. I was using my familiar old .308 Mannlicher carbine, a lovely rifle to be sure but one which, as I would be the first to admit, makes quite a bark. My wife borrowed the estate rifle, also a Mannlicher .308, but fitted with a Reflex T8 suppressor. It was not long before we got into the first group of stags, and I waited behind a large rock while my wife and the stalker went forward to take the shot. I heard the muffled report, of course, and about ten seconds afterwards I observed a line of stags walking away from the scene, stopping every few moments to turn their heads and study with curiosity the place where stalker and shooter were hiding. It was some time before they finally departed, leaving one of their number behind on the grass.

With the gralloch completed, the ghillie summoned and a piece and a dram enjoyed, we set off to find another beast for me. It was not long before we came up to a suitable group of animals on the far side of a heathery ridge up which the stalker and I crawled. With a stag duly selected, I pulled the trigger and the animal went down. At the loud boom of the explosion, however, all hell broke loose and the rest of the group ran as though the very devil was behind them. Same day, same hill, same calibre. Two lots of stags, two different rifles, two totally different reactions from the survivors.

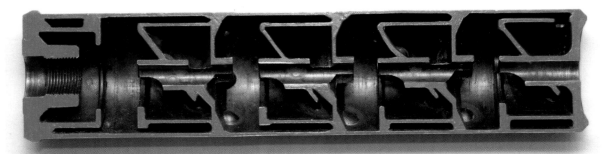

● An Ase Utra jet-Z sound moderator in cross section. The baffles and the threads by which it is attached to the muzzle of the rifle are clearly visible

So how does a sound moderator work? It reduces the muzzle blast from the rifle by redirecting it into an expansion chamber and through a series of baffles. The hot gases are thus slowed down and allowed to cool before they finally exit from the sharp end of the rifle. Remember that a moderator will not reduce the supersonic crack of the bullet once it is in flight. Position yourself (safely) downrange of a moderated rifle and the supersonic crack will be quite evident. What will be far less distinct will be the muzzle blast of the rifle, which of course is the thing that gives away the location of the shooter. A sound moderator will also reduce the rolling echo which an unmoderated full-bore rifle produces in hilly or wooded country.

Moderators come in a variety of different designs, and are either fitted onto the end of the muzzle or are sleeved over the barrel. The latter design, which is fixed both at the muzzle of the rifle and part way along the barrel, offers a more secure attachment. In order to accept a moderator, a rifle must first be threaded. Many new rifles today are factory threaded, but any competent gunsmith will be able to carry out this work on an older firearm.

Benefits of sound moderators not only include the reduction in muzzle blast. They also eliminate the flash which momentarily fills the scope when an unmoderated rifle is fired in low light conditions and which prevents the shooter from observing the reaction of his quarry to the strike. Recoil is significantly reduced, as is muzzle flip. The shooter may also find it easier to distinguish the sound of the strike or impact of the bullet upon his quarry.

There are, however, disadvantages. The biggest gripe I have is that a moderator makes the barrel both longer and more cumbersome, increasing the weight and altering the balance of the gun, making it more difficult to manoeuvre quietly through woodland without getting it snagged in brambles and overhanging fronds. Over-the-barrel moderators will only increase the total length of the rifle by about four inches, but when you are woodland stalking even that short increase in

● A sound moderator is a valuable accessory, but it significantly alters the balance, weight and overall length of a stalking rifle

barrel length can really be quite significant. Furthermore, if the bare metal of the moderator is exposed, then it also makes a tinny 'ping' when struck by leaves or twigs, though this can easily be remedied by covering it with a neoprene sleeve.

Moderators, like rifles, must be looked after. Before the rifle is put away the moderator must be unscrewed, the threads at the end of the rifle barrel lightly oiled and the moderator itself allowed to dry. If the moderator is of a type which can be taken apart for cleaning, then dismantle it, wipe the powder residue from the baffles and the inside of the body with a soft cloth and reassemble it before putting it away. Many moderators are built as sealed units and it is unfortunately not possible to clean the residue from inside them. The best that can be applied to them is a light squirt of WD40 inside the moderator which will help to prevent corrosion. If you leave a moderator on a rifle, particularly after an outing in wet weather, then it will eventually seize to the end of the barrel, requiring the ministrations of a friendly gunsmith to remove it. Almost certainly the threads will be damaged by corrosion and the crown of the rifle may also become pitted. Furthermore, any moderator which is not made of corrosion resistant materials such as stainless steel, or which cannot be dismantled for cleaning, has at best a limited lifespan and will eventually corrode from the inside as it succumbs to the effects of burnt powder residue and absorbed moisture. Eventually one or more pinholes will manifest themselves from which disconcerting puffs of smoke will emanate when the trigger is pulled. It is then time to replace the moderator.

When a rifle and moderator are required for use, the moderator must be screwed firmly (by hand) up to the end of the threads. If it is in any way loose, then the zero of the rifle will be affected, something which I discovered to my cost when I first started to use moderators. No explanation could be found for a worrying series of missed shots until a companion noticed that the moderator of my rifle had become unscrewed by less than a quarter of a turn. Upon re-tightening, the rifle returned exactly to zero. Because it may not be obvious that the moderator has become loosened during the course of a stalking expedition, I now mark my moderator and the barrel of my rifle with small spots of white typist's correction fluid. Provided the two dots are aligned, I know instantly that the moderator is fully tightened.

The only other problem I have with moderators is that they look horrible. I was brought up to love and admire fine firearms and all my life I have enjoyed the look and feel of beautifully oil-finished walnut woodwork, blued furniture and tasteful, understated engraving. Somehow I cannot reconcile the appearance, feel and balance of a traditionally built quality rifle with that of the ghastly looking tube which is stuck on the end of it. Each time I see the lovely lines of a classic rifle thus besmirched I am reminded of that famous observation made by HRH The Prince of Wales about the proposed extension to the National Gallery which he most aptly described as looking like a 'monstrous carbuncle on the face of a much-loved and elegant friend'. But there is a time when one has to choose between beauty and practicality, between the aesthetic pleasures of handling a fine rifle and the workaday requirements of hard usage in the field. At least now the individual shooter has the right to make that decision for himself.

3 Supporting Act

MOST OF US, alongside our rifle, carry at least some means of supporting it when we wish to take a shot. Theoretically it is possible for every shooting position to be unsupported by accessories. Prone shots can be taken off the elbows, sitting or kneeling positions can work very well with elbows braced against knees and of course the standing shot can be taken freehand. And wherever we are in the countryside there are tree trunks, branches, fence posts, stiles and gates; all can be pressed into service to provide support to the rifle when taking a shot, so what is the point of burdening ourselves with unnecessary gear?

If only it were that simple. Admittedly my own hunting philosophy has always been to adopt the minimalist approach. But for the low ground stalker who may well be taking a high percentage of shots from a standing position, stalking without some means of support really is not an option.

Bipods

Those who do a good deal of prone shooting are rarely seen these days without a bipod attached to their rifle. In those pieces of country where there are sufficient contours to make shooting from the prone position a viable option, a bipod is a wonderful aid to accurate shooting. Bipods are almost universally used for zeroing and practising on the range and these days of course you'll rarely see a hill stalker without one. The alternative – a backpack or a rolled up rifle slip stuffed under the forestock to raise the muzzle of the rifle out of heather or grass – still works of course, but there is no doubt that a bipod provides a much

● Bipods are almost universally used for range work when shooting from the prone position

firmer rest, and one which is not going to slip or move as the final adjustments are made.

A bipod is easily fixed to the quick detachable (QD) swivel stud which sits beneath the forestock and a sling can be fitted over the bipod, so it does not in any way affect your ability to carry the rifle. The legs, which fold forwards under the barrel, should snap smoothly, quickly and quietly through 90 degrees into the upright position and be held there by a pair of strong coil springs. Some manufacturers enclose these springs within a rubber sleeve, and this hopefully prevents grass stems or heather getting snagged in them. A hinged or rotating base will accommodate a certain amount of lateral movement between bipod and rifle, thus allowing for any unevenness in the ground and ensuring that the sight picture can be held vertical at all times.

So far as the legs themselves are concerned, these are extendable with either a two- or three-stage draw taking them from around 6 inches to in excess of 27 inches, depending on model. Some designs have notched legs, which extend and lock in prescribed increments, while others are infinitely variable, thus enabling the user to lock each leg off at exactly the height required. It is essential to choose a design that is both simple and above all quiet to use, as you may well have to operate the bipod at very short notice with a wary animal close at hand.

The main disadvantage of a bipod is the weight which it adds to the front end of the rifle, around a pound (450 g) for most models. Not a huge amount, but quite sufficient to compromise the balance of a classic sporting firearm, and there is no doubt in my mind that a bipod, especially when used alongside a sound moderator, makes a rifle more ungainly and cumbersome to use – those comments about monstrous carbuncles spring to mind once more. Given that it can be attached and detached with relative ease, provided that your rifle is first fitted with the appropriate QD swivel studs, there is therefore no need to keep it fixed to the rifle unless circumstances dictate that its use is likely to be required. If you are planning to shoot from a high seat or if you are walking in woodland or thick cover, then remove it. Indeed, I find that when stalking in summer and early autumn when the grass is still high, the opportunities for prone shooting are rare, even when the nature of the ground and the presence of a suitable backstop allows it, though that is not to say that a bipod with long legs might not occasionally be useful when a sitting or kneeling shot presents itself. In winter, however, when ground cover is short, the crops are harvested and the fields are bare, then a bipod is of real assistance wherever there is a regular need to take a shot from the prone position. And of course if you are taking a trip to the open hill, then don't forget to pack your bipod.

● In winter, when ground cover is short and the fields are bare, a bipod is of real assistance to the lowland deer stalker

Stalking sticks

In the great majority of cases, when he is on his feet as opposed to sitting in a high seat, the low ground or woodland stalker will be taking his shots from a standing, sitting or kneeling position, either making use of the best natural rest available or, more likely, shooting off one or more sticks.

Until quite recently the convention was to use a single stick or staff, usually cut from the hedgerow or wood to about the stalker's own height or just a little bit less. A single stick is certainly a great help in steadying the forward hand when taking a standing shot, particularly in helping to control vertical shake. However, it does little to control lateral movement, for which two or more sticks are required to form a bipod or tripod arrangement. By and large, the more sticks, the firmer

● A single stick, like this Bushwear pole, is very quick to use, but offers little control over lateral movement

● A pair of hazel sticks are incredibly easy to deploy and very light to carry. I long ago lost count of the number of deer I have shot off mine

the rest but the more complex it is to set up the sticks and mount the rifle on them, so there has to be a trade-off between the steadiness of the shooting platform and the possibility that in the time it takes to set that platform up, the deer departs for safer pastures.

The simple bipod stick arrangement is still the most popular and lends itself to the production of a really useful piece of home-made kit. When making their own bipod sticks, a lot of stalkers use the green

● When the sticks are well seasoned, lash them together with whipping twine to provide a secure but very flexible joint

● A pair of hazel sticks is an instantly accessible support when taking a kneeling shot

plastic-covered tubular steel garden canes which one may buy at B&Q. They are strong, rigid and two of them may be tied together towards the top to create a very serviceable pair of sticks. Personally, however, I prefer to use natural materials and I make my sticks from hazel rods, usually selected and harvested whilst out stalking.

Two long, straight and reasonably well-matched rods are required, measuring just under an inch in diameter at the base and tapering to perhaps half an inch in diameter at the top, the overall length being that of the stalker's height. It is an enjoyable diversion during a morning's stalk to search for rods of these dimensions in the depths of a hazel coppice, but really good sticks can usually be found, often in the darkest part of the wood, where the young shoots have to force themselves quickly upwards to find the light. Having cut the sticks there and then, or marked them and come back for them later in the day, I season them for at least six months. This is done by fixing them flat and straight against a piece of timber in a cool, dry shed or garage. I knock pairs of staples into the support timber and then bind the hazel sticks firmly into place with agricultural binder twine. Seasoning in this way will take out any twists or bends and ensure that the hazel dries straight.

Once the sticks are well seasoned, I trim them to length and, with a piece of whipping twine, lash them together with a joint which is firm yet flexible, tying off the lashing with clove hitches and cutting away the loose ends. The resulting bipod sticks are incredibly easy to deploy, very light to carry and, most importantly, they introduce no foreign sound to the wood. If knocked, either together or against a tree or branch, they make nothing more than the sound of a hazel rod moving in the wind, which is a thoroughly natural sound in the countryside.

As I have said, I enjoy making my own equipment, but others prefer to buy custom gear from one of the many suppliers of stalking kit, and there are plenty of manufactured sticks on the market, most of them based on a telescopic leg which is adapted from the hill-walker's hiking pole. This is a tubular metal staff with two telescopic sections which turn and lock together, making it possible to adjust the height to suit the individual stalker. Fitted with foam handles at the balance point and at the top, this gadget is available in either a monopod, bipod or tripod format. The latter provides a good stable platform at either standing, sitting or kneeling height. It also enables the stalker to traverse the rifle, thanks to a webbing strap which acts as a cradle to take the forestock. The three pole sticks provide an absolutely solid rest, with none of the back-and-forth wobble which can be apparent when using bipod sticks,

● This adjustable tripod stick from Bushwear provides a good stable platform at either standing, sitting or kneeling height

and because the rifle is resting loosely on the webbing strap, the shooter still retains a wide arc of fire.

Without doubt the most solid rest for the standing shot is the quad-stick or 'mountain staff'. Manufactured from four brown wooden dowels, the unit essentially comprises two pairs of sticks linked to form

⬤ This tripod rest is perfect for tuition on the range

a cradle in which the rifle can sit, with the front support beneath the forestock and the rear one tucked behind the pistol grip. This creates a rock steady rest which controls both vertical and horizontal movement. For carrying, the unit is fitted with a plastic ring that slips over the bottom and a plastic cap that slides over the top to hold the four sticks together. However, removing these accessories to deploy the sticks takes a considerable time and creates a lot of movement, so when walking the woods in expectation of a shot it might well be preferable to have the securing ring and cap already removed. With four sticks, the risk of noise is also multiplied by a factor of four. These sticks feel very secure to shoot from, and those who use them regularly swear that they can be set up almost as quickly as a conventional bipod. I am not so sure, however, and there is a further downside, in that traversing

● This rifleman is using a set of quad sticks. They provide a very solid support when taking a standing shot, but can be relatively slow to deploy

the rifle to left or right, perhaps to track a moving deer, means manipulating, lifting and moving the entire cradle. I know some professional stalkers who use quad-sticks because they offer the most solid and secure of all shooting rests to an inexperienced, possibly nervous guest. Personally, though, I shall be sticking with the rustic simplicity of my twin hazel sticks, at least for the foreseeable future.

4 Assessing Population and Activity

SUPPOSE THAT YOU HAVE BEEN INVITED by a landowner to manage the deer on their farm or estate. They are not unsympathetic to deer and are happy to see the occasional animal about. But what they do not like to see is damage. Damage to their commercial timber caused by browsing and fraying. Damage to their cereal crops and oilseed rape where deer have trampled the fields and lain up in them during the

● Damage to agricultural crops such as this maize is a prime reason for deer management

● Fallow bucks can cause serious bark damage to the stems and branches of trees

day. Slashed and tattered fleece coverings on the vegetable crops where roe have shredded the fabric as they have emerged at dusk from the neighbouring forest.

Perhaps the landowner has important semi-natural woodland on the property in which damage by deer to native plant species is raising official concern within the responsible nature conservation agency. Or maybe the grants that he is receiving for planting new farm woodlands are being compromised by the damage that deer are doing to the young trees.

Can you provide some assistance by controlling the deer? Of course you can, but exactly how many deer should you be shooting, of what species and of which sex and age class? It is a dilemma faced by many a deer stalker when presented with the opportunity to offer long-term management over a substantial piece of ground. Clearly, the stalker has a responsibility to the landowner to put in sufficient time and effort to ensure that the adverse impact of deer on the property is reduced to an acceptable level, but he also has a responsibility towards the deer themselves, for management implies not elimination of the deer – if indeed that were possible or desirable. Instead it suggests a reduction in deer numbers which prevents unacceptable damage but nevertheless leaves a balanced herd. In short, the stalker's object is, or should be, sustainable deer management.

Before deciding how many deer he should attempt to shoot, the deer manager might therefore wish to make some sort of assessment as to how many deer of what species there are on the property.

Obtaining an accurate population census of any wild species is fraught with difficulty, and in the case of deer, one might go so far as to say that it is practically impossible. With the best will in the world there is little prospect of counting each and every animal, even of species which are likely to spend the majority of their lives on the estate in question. With the wider-ranging herding species such as red and fallow, both census and management should ideally be conducted on a much larger 'landscape' scale which, in the case of the lowlands, is likely to range across the boundaries of many farms and estates, both large and small, each with landowners who have slightly differing attitudes towards deer and their management.

Counting deer is difficult, but at least there are a number of recognised techniques which, even if they do not yield a full and exhaustive tally of animals on the property, at least provide a reasonable estimate. Then, if the counting process is repeated over a number of years, that estimate can help to build up a more reliable picture of population change.

Deer can be counted indirectly, by recording what they leave behind in the form of dung, or directly, by observing the animals themselves. Of the two, dung counting is the more economical in terms of time spent in the field, and it also provides an assessment of the average number of animals using a piece of woodland over a period of time, whereas direct counting only offers a snapshot of the number there on the day when the count is undertaken. Furthermore dung counting also provides some clue as to the areas within a wood which are most frequented by deer and the species that have been present there, something which direct counting may not necessarily reveal.

Dung surveys

In order to undertake a dung survey, the deer manager must first mark out a series of permanent plots within the woodland, usually of between fifty and two hundred square metres depending on the density of the woodland and its undergrowth. Some people prefer rectangular plots, whilst others prefer linear plots in which pellet groups are counted a set distance each side of a straight line through the wood. A good idea is to mark trees with an aerosol paint spray to indicate, say, a fifty metre straight line through the wood and then count every pellet group found up to one metre each side of the line. Whether you use a rectangular or linear plot, search out all the pellets within your measured area and either mark or remove them. Then after ten to twelve weeks, revisit the plot and count the number of groups of six or more pellets which have been deposited during the interim period and identify the species involved, making a record of your findings. Counts are best conducted during late winter or early spring, when vegetation is at its lowest and pellet groups are therefore at their most visible.

The number of deer using the wood may then be calculated according to the defecation rate of each deer species: red (twenty-five pellet groups per day), sika (twenty-five pellet groups per day), fallow (twenty pellet groups per day), roe (twenty pellet groups per day) and muntjac (seven pellet groups per day).

Population density is estimated as:

$$\text{Number of deer per km}^2 = \frac{\text{Number of pellet groups per m}^2 \times 1{,}000{,}000}{\text{Number of days between visits} \times \text{defecation rate}}$$

Population density figures achieved in this manner look on the face of it very precise although in truth they can only ever be broad estimates. However, they do serve to give a handle on deer numbers and their usage of a wood. Moreover, the fact that they are arrived at according to an established formula means that they can be compared with figures from elsewhere.

Daytime counting

Counting deer directly by daylight is best done by using a team of helpers or assistants. In a nature reserve where important plant species are being damaged by deer, the members of a conservation society or organisation may well be recruited, but on a private estate the helpers could equally well be beaters on the local shoot.

● When undertaking a daytime count, station experienced stalkers or deer watchers on the downwind side of the wood where they have a clear view

Before the count starts, three or four experienced stalkers or deer watchers, armed with binoculars, are stationed on the downwind side of the wood to be counted, quietly taking up their posts behind trees or bushes, in high seats or in ditches from which they have a clear view of any animals exiting the wood. The helpers then form a line along the upwind side of the wood and walk through it like a line of beaters, at which the counters make a note of any deer leaving the wood. After the beaters have emerged at the end of the 'drive' they compare notes, eliminate any double counting and record the number, species, sex and approximate age of all the deer observed. To this tally will be added any animals seen by the 'beaters' to have broken back through the beating line. In this way a fairly exact total of the number and population breakdown of deer present in the wood at the time of the count can be determined. Again, the count should be repeated in successive years in order that changes both in overall numbers and population composition can be noted.

● Make a note of all deer, like these roe, seen leaving the wood, recording the number, sex and approximate age

Neither of the two counting methods described above requires anything more than good observational and identification skills plus the odd pair of binoculars and a dose of common sense. An alternative counting method can directly reveal a high proportion of the deer on a property, however, it requires access to very expensive thermal imaging technology.

Thermal imaging

Night-time counting by thermal imaging camera makes a direct record of individual animals seen during the course of a drive through an estate during the hours of darkness, when deer have left cover and are feeding or are otherwise abroad in the fields. Ideally the camera operator sits in the back of a pick-up, in an elevated position with a clear view over hedges, fences or any other obstructions, and his camera is linked to a small video recorder and a monitor in the cab. This means that each contact can be recorded and if necessary identified later. Driver and camera operator are linked by radio and ideally the camera operator also carries a handheld GPS unit with which he can record the exact location of each group of deer observed. With a direct line of sight and a good telephoto lens, animals may be

● Deer can easily be spotted at night with thermal imaging equipment. These animals were observed through a Flir Milcam thermal imaging camera and recorded on a digital video recorder

spotted and identified at up to two kilometres by some cameras. A truly remarkable number of deer may be seen at night by these means, with experienced operators sometimes clocking up several hundred animals, especially where large herds of fallow are present, and because no visible lights are used, the deer remain largely unconcerned. Considerable skill is needed to identify the deer species observed and of course to distinguish them from horses, cattle, sheep or indeed any other creatures abroad after dark, but an experienced team can expect to see around a third of all the deer present over a wide area.

Professional thermal imaging equipment is not available from the average stalking supplies retailer and may cost upwards of forty thousand pounds. However, it is the regular stock-in-trade of the Deer Initiative, and landowners in England and Wales with a specific and serious deer problem may, depending on their location, be able to gain access to a thermal imaging count.

Whether it be a dung survey, daytime observation or night-time thermal imaging, a single count will never be sufficient. What is required in each case is a repeated count, carried out at the same time and at the same place over a period of years. If this is achieved, then not only can a broad estimate of population level be obtained, but the success or otherwise of any deer management operation may also be gauged.

Impact assessment

There is an alternative strategy for assessing the size of the cull to be taken which is based not upon deer numbers, but upon the impact they cause. Given that it is the damage, not the deer, which is the problem, assessment of the impact that the deer are having upon their environment is in many ways a more appropriate guide to the extent to which their numbers need to be controlled. If a herd of fallow are present within a wood and yet there is no adverse impact, then there may actually be no need to shoot them. Conversely, if only a few deer are present but they are exacting serious damage to rare or endangered flora or they are preventing regrowth of hazel coppice, then serious control may be required.

● Deer activity indicators:

Top left: A muntjac slot mark

Top right: A dung pellet group. This one demonstrates the presence of sika deer

Bottom left: Slot marks around a deer wallow on a woodland ride

Bottom right: A deer track through ancient woodland

● Deer damage indicators:

Right: Ground flora eaten – a browsed oxlip

Below left: Bark stripped from a larch sapling by roe

Below right: An obvious browse line in old hazel coppice woodland

Bottom left: Bark removed from a woody branch. The height above ground level clearly indicates the presence of red deer

Bottom right: Regular browsing by fallow deer is indicated by the small size of the rapidly re-grown leaves on the lower part of this lime tree

● Deer damage indicators:

Left: Shoots on this ornamental cane have been eaten off by fallow deer

Right: Bark removed from a young tree by fallow deer

Below: Regrowth on this hazel coppice has been eaten off by roe deer

This philosophy has led to the development of deer activity and damage scoring. The technique was originally designed by Dr Arnold Cooke to measure the impact of muntjac upon woodland of high nature conservation value in the east of England, but it has been further refined by Ray Tabor of the Essex Wildlife Trust and shown to be applicable to all species, with a 'total' deer impact assessment being scored. Activity and damage scoring may, to a certain extent, be subjective, but it does not require the services of a trained scientist and can be undertaken by any deer manager who is a competent naturalist.

To undertake a deer activity scoring survey, walk through the entire wood, including the boundary, looking at the frequency with which four indicators are found: sightings of animals, slot marks, droppings and deer paths. To calculate a deer damage score, you should assess a further five indicators: woody shoots eaten off, ground flora eaten, bark removed from woody stems, stems broken down, and an obvious browse line on the vegetation. Using a tick chart, record these indicators as you walk through the wood and at the end of your walk give each indicator a final score of between 0 and 3, according to the following formula:

0	Indicator not present
1	Indicator recorded, but infrequently
2	Intermediate sightings
3	Indicator is abundant

The four activity indicators will give you a maximum score for the wood of 12 and the five damage indicators will give a maximum score of 15.

Scores within a wood can alter considerably from month to month as deer change their feeding patterns with the seasons or use traditional areas for rutting or dropping their young, but as with other survey methods, activity and damage scoring is best carried out in late winter or early spring when it is easiest to observe the various indicators. Repeated assessments in future years enable the deer manager to monitor the level of deer activity and damage, and to see what effect his management is having on the woods. If the scores remain consistently high, then clearly there is a requirement for increased culling pressure, but if the scores fall with culling activity, then the deer manager can gauge the level of his activity to achieve a regular maintenance cull.

Ivy feeding trials

A further check on the intensity of deer feeding activity exploits the fact that fallow and muntjac will selectively browse ivy in the early spring before the emergence of other green shoots. In order to undertake an ivy feeding trial the deer manager will need to cut twenty short ivy stems, each with around thirty leaves and place them straight into the ground one metre apart on a 5 x 4 grid pattern. The stems are then inspected at twenty-four hours, three days and seven days to assess the number of shoots partly eaten and the number defoliated completely.

Rabbits also eat ivy, so if rabbits are present then close inspection is required to identify the cause of the browsing, but if the ivy stems are tied to stakes at sixty centimetres above ground level, then rabbit browsing will be excluded. If the ivy stems are tied to stakes at one metre above ground level then the ivy will be slightly too high for

RESULTS OF ACTIVITY AND DAMAGE SCORES FOR FOUR WOODLANDS IN NW ESSEX – 2003					
Site	Deer species regularly present on site	Activity score	Damage score	% Ivy eaten at 24 hours	% Ivy eaten at 7 days
1	Red, fallow, roe and muntjac	9	10	89	99
2	Fallow and muntjac	6	6	35	30
3	Fallow, roe and muntjac	1	2	6	17
4	Fallow, roe and muntjac	5	4	11	63

muntjac but will be accessible to fallow. Thus an ivy browsing trial can help to confirm which species are present in the wood.

Activity and damage scoring has been successfully used by the Essex Wildlife Trust to assess deer impacts within its reserves and the table above shows how the scores are supported by the results of ivy browsing trials.

In site 1 the deer numbers were very high and not subjected to sufficient control, so both activity and damage scores are high, as are ivy browsing levels. Site 2 showed scores which were about average for the area. Site 3 had a deer fence around its entire perimeter and therefore demonstrated much lower scores. Site 4 had been subject to a high level of deer control for a period of twelve months before the survey (it previously had activity and damage scores of 8 and 10 respectively). The reduction in both activity and damage scores indicates the success of deer management in achieving a more acceptable impact from deer upon the site in question. In woods where there are vulnerable areas of coppice regrowth or sensitive flora, target scores of 3 or below are being aimed at.

Activity and damage scoring systems are quick and easy to use. Though they do not offer any estimate of deer numbers, they do monitor damage levels and if assessments are repeated annually then trends can quite quickly be picked out, giving both the deer manager and the woodland owner clear and scientifically valid information on which to base and to monitor a management programme.

PART 2
IN THE
FIELD

5 Thoughts on Tactics

THEY HAVE, AS AURIC GOLDFINGER FAMOUSLY REVEALED to James Bond, a saying in Chicago: 'Once is happenstance, twice is coincidence, the third time it's enemy action.' These enigmatic words came back to me time and time again as I sat in a high seat one morning, waiting in vain for something to turn up. A high seat is a good place for philosophising about deer stalking because it gives plenty of time both to observe and to think, and as I thought, it struck me that woodland deer stalking is all about turning coincidence into enemy action. Not that the deer stalker is actually his quarry's enemy, though the deer may disagree. But you get the general picture.

In order for a successful shot to be taken, there has to be coincidence of stalker and deer; in other words the stalker has to be at the same place as the deer, at the same time. Imagine that he carefully patrols the wood early one morning, walking stealthily through his beat, moving into the wind in the approved manner and causing the minimum of disturbance with his precisely placed footfalls. In short he is doing everything by the book. At each deer path he gets to, he checks carefully to left and right. He scans each ride and patch of open ground, but after three hours his walk is complete and his vehicle hoves into sight. He has seen nothing and has had a blank morning.

What he didn't know was that just five minutes before he turned the corner of the ride, a roe buck had ambled through one of the areas of clear fell which our stalker was about to patrol. The stalker saw nothing, because the deer had already been and gone by the time he got there. The buck enjoyed an unmolested amble, because between him and the stalker there was coincidence of place, but no coincidence of time. Had the stalker got out of bed or put his boots on five minutes earlier, then he would, by undertaking precisely the same walk, have stood a good chance of a shot. As it was, he saw nothing.

Now let us imagine that the stalker, who has examined the fresh roe tracks through the clear fell and spotted a newly frayed sapling, is pretty confident that the area is regularly used by a particular roe buck. So he decides to stake out the place by erecting a portable high seat with a splendid view of the entire clearing. Wherever the deer emerges within the rectangle of upturned roots, discarded brashings and thin, spindly saplings, it cannot fail to be caught by the stalker's gaze and centred within the reticle of his riflescope. So he selects the perfect spot and fixes his portable high seat. A couple of mornings later he rises early, ascends the ladder of his high seat a full hour and ten minutes before sunrise, and waits. Two hours later, the sun is warming the clear fell, the birds are singing and he still has not seen the buck which, unbeknown to him, has been browsing the edge of another block of clear fell a quarter of a mile away. There has been coincidence of time, but not of place. So still no enemy action, still no successful outcome for the stalker.

So, which tactic is more likely to result in the woodland stalker bagging his buck? Is it better for him to walk, covering as much deer-

● A satisfactory conclusion. This roe doe was taken after a February morning's stalk in the woods

● In summer, when the trees are in full leaf and the vegetation is at its highest, a high seat offers many advantages

friendly ground – within reason – as he can during the course of the morning, or would he be better advised to pick a likely spot and wait in ambush over it, like a leopard lofted in a tree above an African waterhole?

On the whole, I tend to favour walking in the morning and sitting up in a high seat in the evening overlooking a favoured spot at which deer might be expected to appear. However, there are certain factors which might tend to favour one or other of these two tactics. In high summer, for instance, I find that there is little point in stalking muntjac on my feet, for the vegetation is simply too dense to enable me to spot the little

● Through a young spruce plantation on a frosty morning. It is a delight simply to be out in the countryside on such a day

beasties before they spot me, so a high seat situated close to good quality muntjac habitat and within sight of one or more regular muntjac tracks is the only really viable option. Likewise if there is a lot of ground to cover, with none of it representing an obvious honeypot, then stalking on foot at least ensures that everywhere is visited. Even if no deer are seen, there is bound to be an accumulation of information about deer tracks and signs which will add to the hunter's knowledge banks and inform future visits.

Stalking on foot provides a much more varied diet than sitting in a high seat, for you never know what is going to present itself, though by the same token the deer which appears in front of you may not necessarily present a safe shot which is within range. Position a high seat correctly on the other hand, and anything which steps out into the killing zone is liable to be a much easier target, for you have removed some of the variables from the equation.

Some stalkers frankly find sitting in a high seat boring. They point out, with considerable justification, that it is much more interesting to walk for a couple of hours, their hunting skills fully tuned and engaged, than to sit still in the possibly vain hope that something may happen. Moreover they argue that if they see a distant deer, then they at least have the opportunity to stalk it and perhaps get themselves within range, something which may well be impossible to do if they are in a high seat. On the other hand, many of us when culling in woods where there is a substantial measure of public access are virtually obliged to use high seats.

Rain is a disadvantage whether you are planning to walk or to use a high seat. Wind, however, can be an advantage when stalking on your feet, provided it is blowing from a favourable direction. For the high

● In the Norfolk breckland. If there is a lot of ground to cover, then stalking on foot at least ensures that all the most likely spots can be visited

seat shooter, it matters little from which direction the wind blows, so he does, to some extent, have more options on a windy day. He may also have some advantage when it is so still – or frosty – that moving through the woods silently becomes virtually impossible.

On the whole, though, I will always prefer to stalk on a bright morning or evening, perhaps with a bit of frost in the air, and just sufficient breeze to keep the scent drifting in a known direction.

Choice of tactics will also be influenced by land use considerations, cropping patterns and the presence – or absence – of any crop or other food source which deer might regard as a significant draw. Thus a favourite root crop such as carrots or parsnips will prove an irresistible attraction for deer. If you have a field of carrots on the estate where you are stalking and it is the only one in the area, then it does not require rocket science to deduce that this is where the local deer population will congregate at dusk. Walk the surrounding woods and fields by all means, and you may well see them hurrying past in the general direction of dinner. Wait beside the dinner table and they will come directly to you.

In the next two chapters we will take a closer look at the finer points of these two hunting strategies and consider how the woodland stalker can best use them to his advantage.

6 Going on Foot

ALTHOUGH STALKING ON FOOT may not require as much physical organisation as shooting from a high seat, it certainly demands far more mental preparation. One of the great things about hunting wild creatures in their natural environment is that in order to do it well, you have to concentrate fully on what you are doing. The hunting gods are jealous gods, and they will punish those who do not focus entirely upon the signals sent, moment by moment, to the brain by the sensory organs. Ignore what your eyes or ears are telling you and allow the mind to wander in the direction of getting the car serviced, paying the gas bill or even the thought of that breakfast you have promised yourself at the Little Chef on the way home, and you can be quite certain that is the moment when a deer which you should have spotted will jump out from behind a fringe of vegetation and make off into the distance.

Mental concentration is one of the things about hunting sports which makes them such a good way of clearing and refreshing the mind, because for the duration of the hunt, that concentration must be total. I have usually found that, if concentration lapses, then it does so during the final stages of a morning walk, and I can recall several occasions when, in the last twenty minutes of an otherwise blank morning, I have walked into a deer or a group of deer which I should really have spotted. Invariably this has occurred because my mind has wandered from the job in hand, I have gone into 'autopilot' and am thinking about the next item on the day's agenda, whether that is the drive home, a particular job which has to be done later that day in the office or something else entirely unconnected with deer stalking. When I have analysed afterwards what has happened I have usually also found that I have been walking too fast. The best way of avoiding such lapses in concentration is to stop periodically during a stalk, to stand still or sit down on the root of a convenient tree and pause for three or four minutes whilst studying the cover in front and the land round about you with your binoculars and re-focusing your mind on your stalking. When you move off again, do so at half the speed at which you were walking before you stopped.

Planning your route with care is important. Naturally, wind direction has a large bearing upon the ground to be covered, for there is nothing that is more likely to alarm deer than your scent, and it is therefore a basic rule when operating at ground level to work, so far as is possible, into the wind. I usually check the weather forecast before going stalking, to obtain a general idea of predicted wind direction and strength. Then, half a mile or so before arriving at my stalking ground I pull the vehicle into a suitable lay-by or field entrance, get out and make a detailed assessment of the wind. There is a lay-by on a disused airfield quite close to one of my regular stalking areas where I have stopped to check the wind for years. It is far from any trees or buildings, so an absolutely accurate wind check is possible.

Once you have started walking it is, of course, necessary to keep checking and re-checking the wind direction, as it will be affected both by vegetation and basic topography. With a bit of practice it is quite easy to establish when you are facing directly into the wind, especially on a cold day when you can see your breath. In the days when smoking was commonplace, cigarette smoke was always a certain guide to wind direction. Now smoking is less common, some stalkers I know use a squeezable powder puffer filled with talcum powder, while I have seen Swedish hunters pull a scrap of tissue paper from their top pockets, apply a lighted match and immediately extinguish the flame to produce a plume of smoke.

If foot access to your stalking ground is from one point only, then this can well mean that you have to make a considerable detour in order to get yourself downwind of the principal area to be stalked, the time taken to make such a detour being planned into the session beforehand. Keep the detour route well clear of key areas of woodland or cover, for your scent plume can be blown a long way by the wind, and while there should be no need to undertake your preliminary walk at dead-slow stalking speed, especially in the morning if it is still pitch dark and outside legal shooting hours, it is best not to arrive hot, sweaty and agitated at the point from which you propose to start stalking, so allow plenty of time.

There is a wood that I often stalk which runs in direction from north west to south east. Given the prevailing westerly wind, I normally approach it from the south east corner, but when the wind is in the south or the east, I allow an extra twenty five minutes to head a quarter of a mile to the north and make a big westwards circuit around the edges of the adjoining fields to get me to the far end of the wood. Because I invariably stalk this wood in the morning, I try to work my detour into the last twenty minutes before the onset of shootable hours, arriving at the start of my stalk at or just after an hour before sunrise and thus giving myself the maximum amount of stalking time in the place where deer are most likely to be. It's just a matter of checking the forecast wind direction the evening before and timing my departure from home accordingly.

If you are making a detour in order to get the right side of the wind during daylight hours in preparation for an evening session, then don't forget that deer can see you as well as smell you. It sounds obvious, but do remember to make the detour wide enough or use sufficient cover so that animals lurking on the edge of your target area do not catch sight of you as you attempt to get downwind of them. On one occasion I was stalking with a friend and had posted him in a high seat on the edge of a wood in the late afternoon overlooking a field where I knew that roe would emerge at dusk. My own task was to get well downwind and stalk an adjoining block of woodland. It was still early and the winter sun was bright in the sky as my friend slipped quietly into position. Meanwhile, I took a route through the fields some six hundred yards from the edge of the wood, keeping out of sight, or so I thought, under the cover of a hedge. What I had not realised was that even this early in the afternoon, the first roe were already coming out of the wood. 'You know when you went down that hedge,' my friend asked me when we met up after dark, 'Did you see the roe which you spooked back into the wood which I was just about to take a shot at?' He had seen me and so had the roe. Unfortunately I had not seen either of them.

Sometimes deer can crop up when you least expect them, even when you are walking downwind. Suddenly a shape might appear out of the early morning gloom ahead of you or a group of deer might cross your path, perhaps heading for the wood which you are endeavouring to get the 'right' side of. If this happens, I am always prepared to abandon my original plan and change tactics, for a deer in the binos is worth at least two in the bush, probably more. Stand still or, preferably, sink slowly into whatever cover is available and watch the animals carefully, identifying them by species and sex. Are they unconcerned or are they

● Are the deer aware of your presence? This group of red hinds is alert to potential danger

aware of your presence? Are they still feeding or are they obviously anxious to get into cover before it gets light? Are they directly downwind of you or likely to walk into your scent plume? If they are shootable, then is it possible to get downwind of them and make an approach? If they are not, then is it possible to avoid disturbing them, thereby spooking other shootable deer as yet unseen? While I always have a basic plan in mind for the outing, it is never cast in stone and if a potential stalk presents itself then usually the opportunity is worth taking.

When planning an outing it is very easy to drop into a sort of routine in which you walk the same hedge, the same ride, the same wood and glass the same game cover at the same time of day on each and every visit. If that is the only ground open to you then there may be no serious alternative, but if not, then at least consider what other opportunities might exist. An unusual wind direction could favour a different wood, and unless you cover the ground which is available, you will never see the fresh tracks around the edge of the field or the roe hairs clinging to the barbed wire fence on the edge of a young plantation, even if no deer are actually spotted. Indeed, it could be said that if you are not properly covering all your ground then you are not doing your job as a stalker. Intelligence is always valuable, and a word on the telephone with the gamekeeper, farmer or forester the day before your visit never goes amiss. The keeper in particular will have noted any deer he has seen in or about the game crops when he is feeding and watering his birds or on shoot days. Even if he has not seen deer recently, then at least he can advise on any signs of crop damage or, at the end of the shooting season, which game crops have been flailed. A newly flailed maize crop with scattered cobs distributed over the ground is often a magnetic draw for deer, especially because most annual game crops are flailed in February, shortly after the end of the shooting season, a time of year when natural sources of food are at their lowest ebb and any new feeding opportunity is quickly seized upon by wildlife of all sorts.

It may come as a surprise to some, but deer also learn to recognise routine. In particular they very quickly understand if there are areas where they are regularly shot at and other areas where they are safe. When I first started stalking on the farm which I described in the introduction to this book, it was not difficult to see deer there. Even the larger species were not especially wary, indeed they sometimes actually stood there looking at me, and shooting opportunities presented themselves on most visits. Several years down the line, that is no longer true, and while I might like to think that there are simply fewer deer there as a result of my excellent culling, I am not proposing to kid myself that this is the case. The deer are simply more wary. More skill is required to stalk them, different strategies need to be adopted and more hours need to be devoted to obtaining the same level of cull. Some of my stalking friends talk of fields just over their boundaries where herds of deer may be seen peacefully feeding, even in broad daylight. These of course are fields in which the deer are never shot, fields in which they feel safe.

The effect of routine hunting on deer behaviour has been tested scientifically. In one study, biologists observed the daytime vigilance behaviour of roe feeding both during and outside the hunting season and found that roe spent twice as much time being vigilant during the hunting season as they did in the close season. Another study found that during the close season roe selected feeding sites that provided more food but that the animals' behaviour changed during the hunting season when they traded off risk avoidance for food availability. Deer are not stupid. They know when and where they are or are not at risk.

It has occurred to me as I have walked around the English countryside with a rifle over my shoulder that deer, like most quarry species, also have an innate understanding of predatory behaviour. Most of us who spend time in the countryside observing wildlife will have noticed that when we are wearing everyday clothes and strolling along a regularly used footpath, wild creatures will often appear to take little notice of us. They will of course have seen us, the feeding may stop and the heads may come up, but there is no immediate urge to flee. Replace the everyday clothing with hunting kit, carry a gun and creep slowly along the hedgerows, stopping every two or three yards to observe what is going on in the neighbouring fields and woods, and the wildlife will have a completely different take on the human who has invaded their space. This instinctive recognition of predatory behaviour is clear to see if you watch film or video footage of African wildlife. Herds of antelope on the Serengeti show little concern for the pride of lions walking in line astern through their feeding grounds, for they know that the lions intend them no harm. However, should they happen to catch sight of a lioness creeping stealthily through the tall grass, eyes focused and muscles tense, then they will run for their lives.

Afterwards, when one of their number is dead on the ground, being dismembered by said lioness and her family, the antelopes will revert to their feeding behaviour, for they know that the predators have made their kill and that the remainder of the herd, for the time being at least, is safe. You can see exactly the same behaviour displayed by speeding motorists on a motorway: when a police patrol car appears, all the brake lights go on, but as soon as the police patrol has pulled a speeding vehicle over onto the hard shoulder and is busy booking an offender, the rest of the pack resume their former speed.

In planning a route when stalking on foot, I usually pay significant attention to the nature of the ground and vegetation over which I shall be walking. Short grass is the quietest of surfaces to walk on and, other things being equal, that is what I prefer. An uncomplicated surface also means that I can concentrate much more on watching what is unfolding in front of and beside me as I walk, rather than being forced to divert attention towards where I am placing my feet. When walking a lane or track, I either keep to the short grass along the verge or make use of any grass which might be growing in the centre of the track, between the wheel marks, for it is hard to avoid making a noise when walking on a hard metalled, gravelled or stony surface. Mown conservation headlands make good routes for getting about a farm quietly and keeping close to a hedge or field boundary also offers some form of cover. In any event, walking around the edge of a field is almost always better than going across the middle of it, where the stalker is liable to feel horribly exposed, especially in broad daylight. There are, of course, occasions when walking across the middle of a field in daylight is unavoidable, and in those situations you must simply check very carefully with your binoculars before committing yourself.

When in a wood, I try always to use established rides, paths or tracks. Not only do they offer easier, quieter walking which is relatively free of snagging vegetation, but they also provide more forward visibility. It is so much easier to take appropriate action when you spot a potential quarry animal at a distance than when you spot it just a few dozen yards ahead of you. Again, it is better to keep to the edges of the rides if possible, so that cover is available near at hand if necessary. Sometimes, though, there is no option but to strike out through the wood itself, and then it is usually very slow going, for the ground under every footstep must be felt for sticks, twigs or anything else that is liable to make a noise when trodden on, while at the same time you are constantly scanning the wood around you for shapes, outlines, textures or movements that could indicate the presence of deer. Undergrowth and brambles must be negotiated as quietly as possible and account taken of low-growing branches beneath which it is necessary to duck or crawl, noting of course the rifle barrel projecting above your shoulder with possibly a bulky and ungainly sound moderator attached to it. Humans are not the only creatures to walk the woodland floor, however, and there is very often a path which may be picked up, perhaps a deer or badger track. Usually such a path will offer a less complicated route through the wood.

When looking out of cover around the corner of a ride or hedge into an open vista, do so with great caution, inching the binoculars around the obstruction and looking through the foliage or vegetation rather than craning your head around the outside of it. This is made easier if you set the focus dial on your binoculars so that the vista ahead of you is sharp and the vegetation immediately in front of your face is out of focus. Very often hedges or bushes growing out into the edge of a ride or field have a low level browse line as a result of grazing by hares, rabbits or muntjac, so trying to look around them at eye level may not necessarily be a good idea. Although your upper body may be obscured, any observant creature on the far side may be able to spot your legs sticking out from underneath the overhanging bush. So cautiously kneel down and take a look around the next corner from ground level before you commit yourself. Of course it represents extra

● Stalking on foot requires keen observation and total concentration at all times

effort to do so, but when, on your knees, you catch sight of a deer browsing unconcerned just eighty yards down a hedge around the end of which you were just about to emerge, you will agree that the effort was worthwhile.

Binoculars are one piece of equipment that it is virtually impossible to do without when stalking on foot. On a couple of occasions over the course of my stalking career I have left my binoculars at home and it has felt as though I was stalking with one hand tied behind my back or with one eye closed. Good quality binoculars that have been adjusted to suit your eyes will enable you not merely to examine in closer detail objects that are far away, they will enable you to look into the very grain of the landscape. All at once it is possible to see how a falcon or a hawk might feel when studying the ground from aloft with its superior vision. I use my binoculars constantly as I walk, checking in front and beside me while every now and then, when I get to a gap in a hedge or some other viewpoint, I take a longer and more detailed sweep of the landscape. In order to hold the glasses steady, I brace them against my stalking sticks and this enables me to eliminate any shake and thus to check out the middle distance with much more precision. It is stating the obvious to say that binoculars must be properly focused, however, focusing may not be easy in the near darkness of very early dawn, when it is absolutely essential to study the grey and indistinct features around you if you are not to 'bump' your quarry. A useful trick is to focus against the crown of a tree perhaps a couple of hundred yards away. By looking at the topmost twigs or leaves against the slightly lighter grey of the sky you can quickly bring the binoculars into proper focus and, having established the correct setting, you may then use them with confidence at ground level.

Birds can be a huge source of irritation when you are stalking, but they can also provide a clue as to what is happening elsewhere in the wood. Anyone who stalks ground over which there is a busy game shoot will know only too well the difficulty of taking a quiet walk through the woods during late summer and early autumn when they are full of newly released gamebirds. Large numbers of pheasants in

● Binoculars are one piece of equipment which it is virtually impossible to do without

● Bracing the binoculars against your stalking sticks helps to eliminate shake, thereby making it easier to study the middle distance with more precision

the feed rides and on the woodland floor make it extremely difficult to move silently and without disturbing other wildlife, though by the time the shooting season has got underway, things usually get much easier for the deer stalker – assuming that he has the blessing of the landowner and keeper to stalk during the game shooting season. The single cock pheasant exploding with an angry *korrok-kok-kok!* from the undergrowth two feet in front of you as you are painstakingly inching your way through a wood can be enough to give you a heart attack. Strangely enough, though, it does not necessarily mean that every deer in the vicinity is now aware that the deer stalker is on the prowl. I learned that lesson many years ago while stalking roe bucks with one of the Forestry Commission rangers in Thetford Forest. We were creeping along a ride through a block of thicket-stage sitka spruce, with a buck just a bit more than one hundred yards ahead of us. He was moving around in the grass and, this being late summer, he was only partially visible through the waist-high vegetation, so all we could do

● Large numbers of newly released pheasants in the autumn can make it difficult to stalk silently and without disturbing other wildlife

was to wait and see if he would show himself. As we did so, a string of eruptions came from the edge of the ride some fifty yards further on, as a series of indignant cock pheasants burst skywards. The buck took a casual look but appeared to be pretty much indifferent to what was going on, and when a fox proceeded to trot across in front of us, it soon became clear what had caused the disturbance.

● Roe buck and fox: When birds sound their alarm call in the woods, it's not always the deer stalker who is responsible

If I disturb a cock pheasant, then I usually stand stock still for a minute or so, firstly to allow my blood pressure to return to normal and secondly to enable the wood to quieten down, before moving on.

Woodpigeons are a wretched nuisance, though. There are some places where it is virtually impossible to walk quietly without setting off a chain reaction of clappering pigeons rattling out of the trees. First, two or three get up directly over your head, putting every pigeon for fifty yards on the alert. You stand still for a couple of minutes, but the moment you move, the next wave gets airborne and then the next, making it plainly evident to any wild creature that there is a serious predator on the prowl. Small blocks of dense conifers in mixed woodland, or ivy-covered trees along the woodland edge are the worst places for this, and you quickly get to know these favoured pigeon roosting spots. Sometimes the easiest course of action is to avoid them altogether.

However, just as the sound of pigeons and gamebirds can alert other creatures to the possibility that everything in the wood is perhaps not as safe as it should be, so the stalker can likewise learn a great deal from the birdsong around him. The magical sound of a spring woodland, filled with the melody of warblers and finches, the gentle *coo-coo* of woodpigeons weighing in as dawn starts to break, indicates to the stalker that the route ahead is undisturbed and that he is doing his job well. Alarm calls, such as the scolding note of a blackbird or wren, mean that danger has been spotted, and if the calls come from deeper in the wood then perhaps it might indicate that a fox is on the prowl. If they are close at hand, it suggests that the stalker himself needs to take more care.

Occasionally it is necessary to move fast when stalking in woodland, usually in order to reach a position from which you can take a shot at a deer that you have spotted but which looks as though it will be on the move again very shortly. For example I was stalking roe does on cereal fields one morning at the edge of a dense block of young coniferous forestry. The deer had been feeding during the night, and now at first light they were returning to the safety of the forest. From the edge of the trees I could see a doe feeding her way slowly back to cover. Snatching a couple of mouthfuls, looking up and taking a step forwards before putting her head down to feed once more, she was probably 350 yards away when I spotted her and I could see that, assuming she maintained her course, she would enter the wood some 200 yards to my left. I therefore backed off into the forest and, retreating sufficiently far that I could be neither seen nor heard by the deer, I moved to my left as

The results of a successful morning on foot in the woods

quickly and quietly as I could, judging my progress and position by reference to the planting lines of the conifers, beneath which there was of course a dense, quiet carpet of dead needles and no undergrowth to snag my progress. Upon reckoning that I had made the requisite distance, I turned 90 degrees right and crept forward until I could see through the outermost line of trees, to be rewarded by the sight of the doe, now just 150 yards away, still feeding her way quietly towards me. Finding a suitable rest for the rifle, I bided my time until she was perhaps 80 yards off, at which point she turned her head and quartered sideways for a moment. She never reached the trees.

In comparison to the Scottish hill stalker, who operates over open ground with relatively little natural cover except for the undulations in the land itself, the woodland stalker is not required to do a great deal of crawling, but there are nevertheless times when, in order to place himself within shot of a deer, or to reach a position from which he has a safe backstop to shoot against, he must get down on his hands and knees or flat on his belly. This requires a bit of thought and preparation. If I can see the firing point which I have in mind and I know full well that I shall not be needing my sticks to shoot from, then I leave them behind before starting the crawl, as they are an unnecessary encumbrance. My binoculars on the other hand will be required in order to check the position of the animal or animals during the course of the crawl, but if they are left hanging around my neck, they will drag on the ground and become fouled with soil, mud or vegetation, so I slip them under the top of my jacket and zip it up to the neck. On one occasion I forgot to do this when crawling across a light, sandy carrot field to get up to a group of roe. After a long, careful crawl I eventually reached a suitable shooting position and it was only then, when I reached with my right hand for my binoculars, that I realised what I had done, or rather not done. The eyepieces were completely blocked with soil and sand, which had worked its way down into the rubber armouring, rendering the binoculars completely useless. It was weeks before I finally got rid of the last bits of sand and dirt.

As regards managing a rifle during a crawl, I find the most satisfactory method is to carry it on my back, with the sling over my right shoulder and the rifle pulled well across to the left side of my body. This way, the rifle is more accessible than would be the case were the sling to be passed diagonally across my front, though perhaps slightly more unstable if sufficient care is not taken. An alternative approach, but one which I find far less comfortable, is to rest the rifle in the crooks of both elbows in front of me. This works for some people, but because the rifle sticks out on either side of your body as you crawl, there is more risk of it catching on vegetation. Always ensure that the muzzle is kept away from the ground, and on no account drag the rifle by the barrel, thereby potentially allowing vegetation to snag the bolt handle, safety catch or trigger. I know of at least one serious accident that has been caused in this way, with devastating consequences which only by the grace of God did not turn out to be fatal.

7 High Seats

IN COMPARISON TO STALKING ON FOOT, shooting from a high seat sounds as though it ought to be child's play, but of course that is far from the case. High seat shooting is, however, a very powerful strategy for the management of deer. It gives the lone stalker the best chance of a safe shot in a location which deer are known to favour, it offers the opportunity for several rifles to cover a single block of woodland or countryside at one and the same time in a way that would be quite impossible if all of them were to operate on foot, and it enables the busy stalker to make use of the odd bit of time which he might have available without the need to mount a full outing on foot. A two-man high seat is also the perfect way for a stalking guide to introduce a novice stalker to the sport in a safe and controlled environment.

Hunters have always used the ambush as a strategy for taking their quarry, and the high seat is merely a refinement of the ambush principle which offers a comfortable place to sit whilst waiting for a suitable animal to turn up. High seats have long been a primary method of shooting deer in continental Europe, and the traditional Forestry Commission seat, usually sited at the intersection of two principal rides and constructed of poles and timber offcuts, has been with us for decades. Timber high seats are best constructed of treated softwood with one inch thick planking for the floor, though even this has a limited life. The rungs should be bolted or nailed and then wired with galvanised wire to discourage vandalism.

Modern high seats, however, are more usually constructed of steel, which is a far more durable material for a structure which is likely to stand outdoors for several years. There is now a wide range of commercially available manufactured steel high seats in the £200 to £350 price bracket, with several small specialist engineering firms

● A traditional timber constructed Forestry Commission high seat in Shropshire

● Several small specialist engineering firms offer high quality custom built seats such as this comfortable two-seater lean-to

● With this folding seat now fully extended, it is a simple matter to raise it into position against a suitable tree. Note the addition of camouflage paintwork to soften the outline of the ladder

offering custom built seats of very high quality. Obviously it is costly to invest in fixed equipment, but if they are looked after, high seats last for a long time and in situations where deer have to be managed for the benefit of woodland biodiversity, woodland owners can obtain grant aid under the Forestry Commission's Woodland Improvement Grant, which can include the cost of high seat provision. Aid is primarily directed at Site of Special Scientific Interest (SSSI) woodlands which are in unfavourable or declining condition, in which case 80 per cent support for standard costs may be awarded. Owners of non-SSSI ancient or native woodlands may also receive support at a regionally agreed rate. The Forestry Commission 'standard cost' of a galvanised box section steel high seat is reckoned at £300.

When purchasing fabricated steel seats, hot dip galvanising is essential if the seat is to be expected to last, and although box-section galvanised steel does tone down and mellow in time to a dull grey, some stalkers prefer to get out the spray can and treat their seats with

● A free-standing two-seater high seat capable of taking a guide and a guest rifle. Note that the shooting rail could be greatly improved by the addition of a length of high density foam pipe insulation

a coat of olive green paint to make them less visible to the human if not the cervine eye.

If visual camouflage is important, then of even more significance is ensuring that your high seat cannot be heard. I constantly see high seats with a plain tubular steel shooting rail, against which the very lightest touch of a rifle forestock will make a noise sufficient to alert a deer. It only takes the very faintest metallic click for hours of patient waiting to be wasted in an instant. All that is required is a length of foam pipe insulation. Slip this over the shooting rail, bind it in place with fabric tape and the problem is immediately resolved.

Siting of a high seat is absolutely critical, for it is a total waste of your not inconsiderable investment to locate it somewhere which commands

● Temporary siting for a
Deer Initiative portable seat
with free-standing leg kit
during a three day group
cull. The position selected
offers a field of fire over
three rides, which would
have been impossible if a
lean-to seat had been used

a lovely view but is completely off the map so far as the local deer
population is concerned. Look for regular deer paths or tracks, and try
to site your seat within safe shooting distance of several of them –
ideally overlooking the deer equivalent of Piccadilly Circus. The
corners, junctions or edges of rides also provide great visibility, but
having found the right general area you will need to find a suitable tree
to lean your seat against, and unfortunately the best trees are very often
not in exactly the right places to offer the perfect view. If the tree is just
a couple of feet from the ideal position, then visibility, for example
down a ride with regular crossing places, can be lost. This is where a
free-standing seat offers advantages over the lean-to variety, for it can
be moved to precisely the location which is required in order to achieve
the best lines of sight. Many of the commercial lean-to seats can be
supplied with leg kits which make them free-standing at very little
additional cost. When siting a high seat, give some thought to
prevailing wind direction, because although this may not be much of
an issue once you are sitting in it, you will almost certainly want to be
able to stalk in to your seat unseen and undetected. Furthermore, if you
are planning to use the seat throughout the year, especially in
deciduous woodland, imagine before you install your seat what the
wood will look like both with and without a canopy of leaves or tall

● When setting up a lean-to seat, don't neglect to fix a retaining strap or rope around the tree

ground cover in the rides. Access is also important, especially if you are proposing to erect chunky bits of metal or timber that will need to be brought in on the top of a 4x4 vehicle.

Bear in mind that forests change, sometimes quite quickly, and yesterday's coppice coup, filled with succulent, tempting shoots issuing forth from the newly coppiced stools, is tomorrow's block of dense woodland. I can think of several high seats, mostly old permanent wooden ones, which must once have been in excellent locations but which are now to all intents and purposes useless, simply because the woodland around them has changed.

Having said that, the life of a high seat can be prolonged with a bit of judicious trimming of nearby branches and even the cutting of shooting lanes – with the landowner's permission of course. A small bush saw or bow saw is an essential tool to carry when setting up high seats.

● Choosing a site which is accessible with a 4x4 vehicle saves a great deal of hard work when setting up a new high seat

● A new coppice coup is susceptible to damage by roe deer, but is effectively overlooked by this seat. Note the importance of clearing brush away from the foot of the seat and the path leading to it, in order to ensure quiet access for the stalker

⬤ This Forestry Commission high seat has a commanding view over a large area of newly planted woodland

⬤ Mineral licks can be used to draw deer. This mineral block is sited on a pole so that it cannot be trashed by deer, yet the salt from it will wash down the pole whenever it rains

Some stalkers even manage to improve the habitat around favoured shooting locations by sowing attractive food plants or possibly a commercial deer lawn mixture containing a range of palatable grasses, clovers and specially favoured plants such as perennial chicory. A well balanced mixture will provide good levels of protein and minerals and is usually designed to be sown in woodland rides or clearings. Such crops and mixtures are available from specialist merchants of conservation crop seed. A more temporary draw can be achieved by the use of small piles of root vegetables such as carrots, or alternatively by using mineral lick blocks. I have also found proprietary salt paste to be helpful in some situations, when smeared on a suitable tree stump around ground level. Does it actually attract deer? I really don't know, but all it has to do is to make a muntjac hesitate for a moment, stop and put its head down to take a lick as it walks across a ride, and the salt has done its job. It has certainly achieved that much for me, on more than one occasion.

Where there is public access to woodlands, then shooting from high seats as opposed to stalking on foot can become a necessity for safety reasons. Of course no sane stalker will take a shot without an absolutely safe, clear backstop, but basic geometry dictates that the angle of incidence of a bullet fired from an elevated position towards a target two feet or so from the ground will offer a backstop which is closer behind the target than would be the case if the shot were taken from

● Where woods are accessible to the public, it is advisable to fix warning notices to high seats

● This portable folding seat, constructed of box-section aluminium, can be erected and installed within minutes, even in the dark

ground level. Certain conservation bodies that manage deer in their publicly accessible woodland reserves, quietly and without fuss, insist that their stalkers operate from high seats, while the same applies to some Forestry Commission sites. Public access does bring its own risks for expensive fixed capital equipment, however, and it is not unknown for high seats to be vandalised or stolen by members of the public who somehow think that they are doing the deer a favour. Regrettably it is not only the animal rights fringe who will steal high seats: some unscrupulous deer shooters – one hesitates to call them deer stalkers – have been known to steal high seats either for their own use or for sale to other shooters who are prepared to buy without asking too many questions. Thus it makes sense to locate high seats well away from main public access routes, and it may be necessary to chain and padlock them to trees. At the very least a warning notice should be appended to deter members of the public from climbing into them.

Another option in situations where the stalker does not want to leave valuable equipment in the woods for long periods of time is the portable folding high seat. These excellent products represent one of the most useful pieces of kit the serious stalker can buy. A German-made seat, manufactured from box-section aluminium, with a moulded plastic seat and weighing less than thirteen kilograms, has been around for several years. It is light and portable enough for a stalker to carry on a strap over his shoulder and can be erected and installed against a suitable tree within minutes. It is even possible to erect the seat in the dark and, with a bit of practice, in almost total silence. Now the German seat has been copied in the Far East, thereby bringing down the price of this really useful accessory. With the addition of a leg kit to make the unit free-standing, these seats are even more useful to the deer manager.

A portable high seat is not merely a valuable aid in situations where there is a risk of theft or vandalism, it is also the perfect method of assessing the suitability of potential high seat locations before setting up more permanent structures. Furthermore, portable seats are ideal when a number of shooting locations are required on a short term basis, such as for the duration of a team cull, or for dealing with a temporary situation in which marauding deer are causing crop damage on a particular field.

So how do you shoot successfully from a high seat? Is it not just a case of climbing a ladder, waiting for a deer to appear and then pulling the trigger? Well not exactly. Assuming the seat is well sited, the first task is getting to it quietly and without disturbing any deer or other animals or birds that may be close by. There will inevitably be occasions when there is an animal close to the seat as you approach it, so if the timing of your visit is during shootable hours, then stalk in to the seat carefully, and preferably from the downwind side.

Rifles should be unloaded before climbing, because slips and accidents can happen, even with the most experienced users, but when you are in position and seated, do remember to load your rifle afterwards. There are few things as exasperating as lining up on a shot for which you have waited perhaps a couple of hours and squeezing the trigger, only to find that you have failed to insert a magazine or chamber a round.

If using a seat for the first time, adjust the shooting rail, if it is adjustable, to a height that suits you and which offers appropriate support to a potential shot taken in the direction from which an animal is most likely to appear. Remember that if it is too high or too low, then you cannot start altering it when there is a deer in front of you, and an

● A length of hessian scrim provides additional concealment to the occupant of this high seat

● With its circular shooting rail, this seat offers comfortable shooting over a particularly wide field of fire. Note the galvanised steel legs which make it free standing

uncomfortable shooting position is liable to contribute to inaccurate shooting. Make sure that the rail is rock steady, as a good, solid rest will enable a shot to be taken right out to your personal limit of confidence.

By all means take a look around with your binoculars, noting landmarks which can be used to judge range, but there is usually no need to make constant use of binoculars once you are in position. The average pair of human eyes is quite capable of picking up the movement which will indicate the emergence of an animal into the field of vision, and only then should it be necessary to use the glasses to confirm identification. Constantly raising and lowering the binoculars is liable to create unnecessary movement which can so easily give away your position. Likewise I try to keep head movement to a minimum, while of course ensuring that the ground is properly scanned.

Ensure that you are clad sufficiently warmly. Two hours or more of total inactivity halfway up a tree at dawn on a cold January morning is a test for the hardiest of souls and even an evening session in late

● A fully enclosed cabin designed to keep out both the rain and the Scottish midges

summer can see temperatures drop sharply after sunset. When high seating in winter I go for the full rig of long underwear, padded overtrousers and a body warmer over the fleece I usually wear under my stalking jacket. A great deal of body warmth may be lost through the top of the head, so don't forget to wear a well-insulated hat or cap.

One of the principal benefits of using a high seat is that the stalker does not have to worry about wind direction. His breathing will produce a plume of scent which drifts downwind, but this plume will be above the level at which the deer can intercept it. However, because you are perched up in a tree several feet off the ground and deer may not be able to wind you, it is quite easy to assume that they cannot see you either. Of course that is not necessarily the case: just because you have climbed into a high seat does not mean that you have instantly been rendered invisible. A careless stalker may be spotted even in a lean-to seat tucked cosily into the branches of a tree, and when sitting in a free-standing seat on flat, open ground at the junction of two rides he can be seriously exposed. Timber cladding on a permanent seat will offer visual concealment and a certain amount of protection from the weather, while there are even high seats on the market with an enclosed cabin which is designed to keep out the rain and the Scottish midges. However, the best strategy is to keep quiet, still and alert. If and when a shootable animal is seen, then movement with the rifle should be slow and steady, for it is all too easy to spook a deer by raising or manoeuvring the rifle too quickly, especially in full daylight when the animal is relatively close at hand. Obviously there is more latitude in low light and with deer that are at longer range.

There is rarely any opportunity for taking liberties with sound, except perhaps in a strong wind. Deer and other wild creatures will pick up any unnatural noise at a surprising distance, even something as faint as the sound of a clumsily released safety catch. Wild boar in particular have the most incredibly acute hearing and I remember losing my first chance at a pig, when shooting from a high seat in Lithuania, simply by pushing the safety off too quickly. The sound that was made when I slid the button forward a little over-hastily in my relief at seeing a beast in front of me in the clearing was barely audible, but it was enough to send that sow bolting for the forest. Thankfully for me – and the old forester who was guiding me – a second animal emerged some ten minutes later whilst it was just still light enough to shoot, and this time I was more careful with the safety catch. On another occasion I was waiting for a Chinese water deer on the edge of a marsh in Norfolk. I was sitting in a high seat which had a plain galvanised shooting rail, with no padding on it of any kind. It was very early in the morning that a buck emerged from the boggy wood beside me and as I manoeuvred my rifle into position I touched the shooting rail with the forestock. It was no more than the lightest of touches, but in the stillness of dawn that CWD heard it and took off like greased lightning. At a range of two hundred yards it stopped and lay down in a bed of sedge and rushes. I glued my eyes to that spot for a full twenty minutes during which I don't believe I as much as blinked. Eventually the buck felt safe enough to stand up, which was lucky for me but unlucky for him. I succeeded in the end, but had I not been clumsy when the animal walked out of the wood, it would have been a far easier shot.

After having taken a successful shot, there may be no absolute need to come down out of your seat, especially when the objective is to get a number of deer in the larder. Even when you are using an unmoderated rifle, it is worth remembering that in some situations, such as arable farming areas where there are gas bangers going off repeatedly throughout the daylight hours, deer do not necessarily worry overmuch about loud bangs. I have often shot a muntjac from a high seat, only to have a second animal walk out in front of me minutes or even seconds later. Provided that I can see clearly that the first animal is dead, I will usually bide my time in the hope of shooting another rather than blowing any chance of a second opportunity by climbing down to the ride and getting on with the gralloch.

On some occasions a stalker is more or less committed to staying in a high seat for the duration of his outing. Obviously this is the case when he is under instructions from the deer manager, forester, hunting guide or other supervising person, or when the conditions of his stalking permission demand it, perhaps in a public access woodland. But in other situations it can be beneficial, or more enjoyable, to sit for part of the outing and walk for the remainder. Often it is best to sit in a favoured spot when the light is at its lowest and walk when the light is better, so a morning session might involve getting into a high seat before it is light enough to shoot, waiting there until sunrise and then going for a walk. Conversely in the evening I will sometimes stalk on foot until dusk approaches and then head for a high seat situated at a spot where I know that deer are likely to emerge at last light into a favoured feeding area. If possible, I have a number of high seats in place: one or two permanent ones and a couple of portables which can be moved around. This offers excellent flexibility for different wind directions and adds variety and enjoyment to my stalking outings. It also enables me if required to put a guest in one seat and then stalk on to another.

Although a high seat is the conventional accessory with which to mount an ambush, it is not always necessary to situate yourself above ground level. The 'low seat', a form of shooting hut with apertures to the front and sides through which a shooter may point his rifle, is popular in continental Europe and can be a discreet and useful aid to covering particular pieces of ground which deer habitually use. For example a 'low seat' might be sited on one side of a valley, usually downwind of the prevailing wind direction, to cover a favoured spot on the opposite side. Some stalking equipment suppliers even offer portable hides which can be used in much the same way.

● Where there are natural contours in the land, a low seat or 'doe box' can be a useful aid to covering a piece of ground that deer habitually use

However, the stalker can quite easily take advantage of whatever cover is available to him, especially when managing temporary situations, such as when deer are raiding a particular crop. Straw bales are an obvious form of concealment, but the stalker can just as easily shoot from a suitably situated pile of pallets, a sugar beet clamp or – less attractive – a well placed manure heap. Alternatively he might be able to persuade the farmer to park a farm wagon in a convenient spot. Otherwise he can simply lie out in the field and wait, for example when deer are emerging at dusk from woodland to feed on root vegetable fields. Naturally reconnaissance is required, and it is essential to spend time on the field during the day to establish exactly where the deer are feeding and where they are emerging from the wood. Their slot marks and the evidence presented by bitten or half eaten roots will quickly direct you to the hot spot, and then it is a matter of considering wind direction, acceptable range and, most important, safe backstops.

I have repeatedly played this game over the years, perhaps during spells of two or three evenings when it can become like a game of cat and mouse. On the first night, when you think that you are in the right place, the deer emerge from a location which you hadn't spotted, which is out of range or where there is no prospect of a safe shot. But at least you can estimate how many animals of what species are using the field until, under cover of darkness, you quietly back off leaving the deer undisturbed. Perhaps the following evening the wind has changed, making the stake-out impossible, until finally the evening comes when you get it right and are able to get one, two or even more animals in the larder.

8 Calls and Calling

THE USE OF CALLS in woodland stalking can be either spectacularly successful or a complete waste of time. That said, I always carry a call in the left hand side pocket of my stalking jacket and it is surprising how often it gets used.

In the context of British deer stalking and the European tradition from which many of our practices derive, the use of calls is principally associated with roe deer, calls being classically designed to produce a squeaking sound which will attract the roe buck at certain times of the year. The devices themselves fall into two principal categories: those you blow into and those that you squeeze. The former come in a bewildering variety of different shapes and sizes and take a good deal of practice to master, but once you have learned how to use them they can have the advantage of leaving both hands free. Provided you have the call attached to a lanyard which is placed around your neck, it is possible to hold the call between your lips or in your teeth like a dog whistle and to make a variety of sounds whilst at the same time having both hands on the rifle. Many of these calls can also be adjusted or 'tuned' to vary the pitch of the note that is produced.

The alternative is a call which has attached to it a rubber bulb that you squeeze in order to force air through the sound-producing reed, such as the hugely popular Buttolo call. This is a truly excellent and highly versatile call, which can be made to emit a wide vocabulary of different notes and sounds, from a quiet, plaintive bleat through a more urgent squeak to, if the bulb is depressed sharply, the 'rape' call of a roe doe. Obviously it requires a free hand to operate it, so if the stalker wants to work the call to move or draw in a deer that is a short distance ahead, he must either be prepared to let go of the call at the critical moment to get both hands on the rifle, or to work the call with one

● The popular Buttolo call alongside a continental 'whistle' type roe call which may be held between the teeth when in use

hand and shoot with the other. This is not as impossible as it might seem, provided that the rifle is fitted snugly on a pair of sticks or some other rest and the shot, as is usually the case, is being taken at close range. One disadvantage of the Buttolo is that it tends to be rather loud, so it is often a good idea to hold it in your pocket when using it in order to mute the sound. Lifting it out of the pocket for a couple of squeaks and then re-inserting it to vary the volume can generate an interesting variety of sounds. While most stalkers opt for a proprietary call, a wide variety of squeezable squeakers can be pressed into service, and I know at least one stalker who uses a small squeaky child's toy to great effect.

Further varieties of call include the natural products of the countryside, such as the highly traditional beech leaf of the German *jäger* or the blade of grass which is stretched between the middle thumb joints of two cupped hands. Crude, but actually quite effective – I have known the sound produced by a blade of grass to draw a muntjac in to less than thirty yards.

Whilst considering calls, let us not forget those which are used in the US to draw a range of different deer species to the rifle. American deer hunters, like their British and European counterparts, use mouth-operated calls, most notably for reproducing the grunting or 'bugling' of the elk, while some US hunters also carry rattling devices designed to imitate the sound of two male deer, antlers locked together, engaged in combat. More controversial to British ears is the use of electronic recordings to attract deer. Such devices, which play back recorded calls, are widely advertised in Britain as being suitable for attracting deer for the purposes of observation and photography. In fact the 1981 Wildlife and Countryside Act does not prohibit their use for decoying deer to the rifle in the way that it prohibits the use of electronic calls to kill or take wild birds, and the use by deer stalkers of electronic calls is actually perfectly legal in Britain. Whether or not it is regarded as ethical is quite another matter. It is highly likely that many sporting deer stalkers would regard the use of an electronic call as 'not the done thing', but the deer manager who needs to use every trick in the book to achieve his cull in the dying days of the season might take an entirely different view. Ultimately the decision on questions of ethics such as this must lie with the individual hunter.

Turning from a review of the calls themselves to a consideration of the way in which they might be used, it is convenient to divide the calling of deer into two categories, the strategic and the tactical. In the one case, the stalker deliberately sets out to use a call in order to attract

● An inquisitive roe buck. When everything goes right, a buck can be upon you seconds after the call is used

● When calling muntjac it is often a doe that will show herself first. The buck may not be far behind, but this doe is obviously pregnant and would be a good animal to cull

deer, picking a suitable location and positioning himself and his equipment accordingly. In the other, he might use a call to conjure a shot out of the hat when a deer is already in front of him. This is not unlike the sharp whistle which one might use to stop a moving deer or even the waving of a stick in the heather by the highland stalker who wants to get the recumbent stag to stand up.

Looking first at the strategic, the classic use of a call, at least in Europe, is to draw a roe buck during the rut by fooling him into thinking that there is a doe in oestrus close at hand. This can be achieved by imitating either the sound of a young kid, which will not be far from its mother at the time of the roe rut, or the 'rape' call of a doe under pressure from a buck. In suitable conditions, such as sultry, humid or thundery weather when the rut is at its height, either note can be devastatingly effective, bringing a buck in front of you within seconds. Or more often it can be a complete waste of time.

Calls can also be used very successfully to attract other species. I have occasionally called fallow, on one notable occasion in late summer bringing a doe trotting up the edge of a wood to within a few feet of where I was lying on a grass margin. However, my most frequent success has been with muntjac, and because muntjac are year-round breeders, there is not the strict element of seasonality in calling muntjac that there is with roe. Here, the trick is to imitate the bleat of a fawn in distress, a sound which will attract any nearby adult animal to see what the fuss is about and, perhaps, to intervene and drive off the presumed predator. In my experience the first animal which comes to the call is usually the doe, and if this happens then a judgement can be taken over whether or not to shoot, depending upon the animal's pregnancy status. But continued use of the call will often demonstrate that the buck is not far behind.

If you wish to call muntjac, then position yourself on the downwind edge of suitable woodland, bearing in mind that muntjac will always try to get downwind of you in order to try and work out exactly what you are. Pick a leafy bush or tree, such as a holly, to stand in front of and thus break up your outline. Put your rifle on sticks or some other suitable rest and face into the wood so that you can see for perhaps forty yards through the trees with dense cover beyond, remembering that when responding to a call, a muntjac will always avoid crossing open ground. A sequence of seven squeaks repeated at two minute intervals seems to work, and I have occasionally had muntjac upon me within seconds. Surprisingly, the technique can also work when you are sitting in a high seat, for muntjac don't seem to worry that the sound is apparently coming from halfway up a tree. However, calling is not a strategy that should be over-used in the same piece of woodland, for I have little doubt that deer, like other species, will quickly become call-shy if they learn to associate the sound of a call with the presence of a human predator. Furthermore, although we try of course to get the notes accurate, I often wonder whether on occasions we might, without knowing it, make some appalling gaffe in deer vocabulary.

The most obvious tactical use of a call is to stop a deer which is walking or running, thereby making a shot possible, though in these circumstances it is usually the case that a whistle, bark or even a shout is quicker and easier than reaching into a pocket for one's trusty deer call. However, there are situations when a little more time is available in which a call becomes a really useful aid. Tactical use of calls can be very effective if a deer is close at hand and you wish to draw it out of

⬤ When calling deer, select a position with a solid background which is downwind of the cover from which an animal is expected to come, and position the rifle on a rest. Shooting one-handed will enable you to work a Buttolo call, muted in a side pocket, while avoiding any unnecessary movement when it is time to squeeze the trigger

dense cover to a place where it can be seen more clearly. An example might be where a deer has crossed a ride in front of you and gone into cover. If the rifle is set up on sticks and a couple of squeaks are made with the call, then it may be possible, if the animal is inquisitive enough, to get it to turn round and step back out into the ride to see what the fuss is about, and I have successfully used this tactic with muntjac on a number of occasions. A couple of squeaks can make an animal step out of the undergrowth and show itself even if it has run into cover at your approach, provided that it has merely moved there out of caution at the arrival of an unspecified threat and has not been alarmed by the immediate intrusion of a human being and hightailed it into the next parish. Even when a muntjac is standing in cover, barking at what it obviously recognises as a potential danger but one which it has not perhaps identified as a human, I have on occasions been able, with the aid of a squeaker, to draw the animal sufficiently towards me to get a clear view of it and so take a successful shot. To do this you must again set the rifle up on sticks, facing the direction of the barking, watch the undergrowth for the slightest glimpse of the muntjac and have a lot of patience.

Very occasionally when stalking deer I have used a call 'in reverse'. That is to say I have been guided to the shot by the sound of the animal's calling rather than luring it to me by the use of an artificial call. During the fallow rut, for example, the groans and grunts that echo through the trees in the early morning can be used as a guide to which rutting stands are occupied by bucks, and the same principle may apply also to the unearthly roar of rutting red stags. However, I have had some of my most fascinating stalks on vocalising deer when stalking muntjac. Such a stalk can only be achieved when a muntjac barks for a long period because there is a territorial rival – or perhaps a potential mate – close at hand to which it is announcing its presence. Naturally you have to be downwind of the barking animal when you first locate it, and you also have to know the geography of the wood in great detail, so that you can make a fairly exact guess where the target muntjac is located, together with all the rides, tracks, glades and denser areas of vegetation which surround it. With a bit of practice and a detailed knowledge of the layout of your wood, it is not too difficult to estimate the range and direction of a barking muntjac down to a few yards, pinpointing it to a particular location. If all the circumstances are in your favour, then the initial approach can be made quite quickly, but over the last couple of hundred yards you reduce your pace to the slowest imaginable, scanning every square inch of tree trunk, stem, leaf and coppice stool for the muntjac which you can hear barking just in front of you. Bear in mind that the deer may not be static, but may actually be walking round in small circles as it barks, hopefully providing you with the opportunity to catch its movement against the surrounding vegetation. When it all comes together, stalking by sound at a barking muntjac is unbelievably exciting and demands every last bit of concentration.

9
Cometh the Hour

'SUBJECT to sections 6 and 8 below, if any person takes or intentionally kills any deer between the expiry of the first hour after sunset and the beginning of the last hour before sunrise, he shall be guilty of an offence.'

The Deer Act 1991, like its counterpart in Scotland, the Deer (Scotland) Act 1996, is quite specific about when the deer stalker may and may not go about his business. When planning a visit to the woods, if I have not been stalking within the previous couple of days, I normally check the BBC weather website for the local times of sunrise and sunset so that I can plan my arrival accordingly, remembering that these times vary quite dramatically according to both longitude and latitude. But, given that there is a clear legal window within which shooting may take place, when is the best time to start and to finish stalking operations?

Some years ago a Somerset stalker, Norman Brade, who had recorded in great detail the times of day at which he had taken his shots, analysed his personal records and had the resulting statistics published in the BDS journal *Deer*. He found that over a period of five years of stalking records, the average time at which he shot his roe deer – bucks and does alike – was one hour ten minutes after sunrise. The latest time he recorded was two hours twelve minutes after sunrise and the earliest was eighteen minutes before. This intriguing analysis might indicate that there is little value in stalking during the first thirty minutes of legal shooting time and that the stalker might just as well spend an extra half an hour in bed. If my experience is anything to go by, however, such an approach would mean an awful lot of missed opportunities.

The earliest shot I can remember taking occurred one year on 30

● It is always worth getting up just that little bit earlier so as to catch deer, such as this fallow buck, out in the woods at the first grey glimmer of daylight

August. As usual I had checked the time of sunrise and confirmed this to be at 6.03 a.m. in the part of east Suffolk where I was stalking. As it was late summer, the woodland vegetation was still dense and the grass in the rides was tall, making it difficult to see much from ground level, so I was planning to use a high seat. I aimed to be in the high seat shortly after five o'clock and the Radio 2 pips went as I parked the Land Rover on a ride which would give me just a short walk in to the seat. I was already dressed in my boots and overtrousers, so it did not take me long to put on my stalking jacket, gloves and head net, remove the rifle from its slip and pop in a loaded magazine, and I set off in almost total darkness, just the faintest smudge of grey showing through the heavy canopies of the oaks above me.

After two hundred yards, however, when I stopped and scanned the path ahead of me, I could see what appeared to be a deer grazing under the heavy shade of a mature cypress tree which stood at the side of the ride along which I was walking. The glasses confirmed it to be a muntjac buck, broadside on and in perfect silhouette, so carefully I set up the sticks and brought the riflescope to bear. The deer was visible through the 8 x 56 Schmidt & Bender scope of my .243 even though it was too dark for me to see the illuminated reticle, which I had foolishly forgotten to turn on when I had left the vehicle. Incredibly the animal stood still while I powered up the scope to provide me with a pretty red dot to place on its chest. I squeezed the trigger and heard a satisfying thump at what I estimated to be about 5.05 a.m., a case of the early muntjac catching the bullet.

On the whole, however, shots at muntjac tend to be much later in the morning than that. I often find that it is worth waiting long after sunrise before heading for home at the end of a trip, for often a muntjac may be spotted wandering along a hedge or across a ride in the warming rays of the morning sun long after it has risen. Of all the deer species that I regularly stalk on low ground, the muntjac is the one which presents shooting opportunities across the widest time bracket. Their small size means that they have to feed more often than other species and muntjac are active for about 70 per cent of the day, with an average of five three-hour foraging periods spread throughout the twenty-four hours. It is possible to come across them at quite literally any time of day, but I usually make a point of looking for them both an hour and a half after sunrise and, if I am on an evening outing, from a couple of hours before sunset, especially on a warm, sunny afternoon, for they are more active in warm weather.

On many occasions at the end of a morning stalk I have gralloched a deer shot before sunrise and have been dragging or carrying it back to my vehicle when a muntjac has walked out in front of me. Usually at this stage of the stalk I have my hands full, making a shot impossible. But not always, and I have learned to be on my guard until the moment I arrive back at the vehicle for the animal, usually a muntjac, which steps out in front of me long after dawn.

Fallow, on the other hand, tend in my experience to be early birds, and especially the bucks. If I want to catch a fallow out in the open, I find that I really need to be on site well before the very first glimmer of dawn to allow myself sufficient time to commence stalking at the first available moment of legal shooting time. Even then, I have occasionally been rewarded with no more than the backside of a buck heading back across a field into the stygian gloom of the wood from the maize cover crop where he has been feasting during the hours of darkness. On one occasion I even surprised two bucks munching by moonlight on the

Brussels sprout patch in a cottage garden as I headed towards the wood which I was intending to stalk. I was as startled as they were, and they quickly made off. Even had it been within legal shooting hours, it would have been inappropriate to have taken a shot beneath the bedroom window of the cottage, irrespective of the fact that I knew the occupants to be well disposed towards deer stalking. Fallow does seem to hang around in the open a bit longer than the bucks, but it is rare that I see one out and about much after half an hour before sunrise.

Like all other species, fallow become more wary and spend less time abroad during daylight hours as the season progresses. By late autumn

● In some places, as a result of shooting pressure, fallow have become almost entirely nocturnal in their habits

it seems that in many places where they are hunted, fallow only emerge from the woods under cover of total darkness and return before the first glimmer of dawn. During extended three or four day midwinter culls I have had high seats fully manned throughout morning and evening shooting hours to little effect despite the fact that substantial numbers of deer are known to be using the area. That the fallow have been abroad by night has been evident from the slot marks at first light in the wheel-tracks my Land Rover made when I was setting out high seats the previous afternoon.

In circumstances like this, the only effective remedy is a great deal of patience and a willingness to devote long hours to the cull. Theoretically, it might be possible for a landowner who is suffering serious deer damage to obtain from Defra a licence to shoot at night. In practice, however, to obtain such a licence he would have to demonstrate not merely that the damage itself is serious but that alternative courses of action, namely deterrence and shooting during legal hours, have been unsuccessful. Such licences are granted only on very rare occasions.

There are a number of factors that govern the choice between stalking at first light and making an outing in the evening, not the least important of which are the stalker's other commitments and his work patterns. For those lucky enough to have their home, their stalking area and their workplace geographically close together, then in the summer months at least it is quite feasible to slot in a stalking trip early in the morning and to be completed in plenty of time before the working day commences. However, one must always be prepared for the unexpected, and finding a lost animal or dealing with a particularly large dead one can take a great deal more time than might have been anticipated.

Morning in the countryside is usually a quiet time, and to be out and about before the rest of the world has awoken, before farm machinery is started up and before the hum of commuter traffic gets going on the local roads, is always relaxing. The stalker can share the fields, woods, hills and hedgerows with the birds and wild animals, and hopefully with the deer. In spring there is the added delight of the dawn chorus, which starts in the woods before it gets light with the luscious, liquid notes of the nightingale and the hooting of the tawny owl. Then, in that magical time midway between night and morning as the light level slowly rises, the other birds chime in – the cooing woodpigeons in the higher branches, the willow and wood warblers, then the robin, blackbird and chaffinch. Perhaps, if you are lucky, you will hear the

● Morning in the countryside is a quiet time when the stalker can share the woods with the deer and other wild animals

unmistakable sound of the cuckoo. It is a sad and sullen human spirit which is not lifted by such a virtuoso performance.

Deer are relatively undisturbed by human agency at this time, allowing two or even three hours of potentially uninterrupted stalking at the beginning of the day. On balance, the same cannot be said for the evening, when the human world is active, when traffic is busy on the roads and people are walking their dogs. Often it is only in that last half hour or so before total darkness that deer will, if the stalker is lucky, steal quietly out of cover and make their way to that night's favoured feeding place.

But although deer may not actually show themselves until the light is almost gone, they can often be gathering at a favoured secure location for some time beforehand. So it is therefore essential for the stalker contemplating an evening ambush, from a high seat or some other fixed position, to be ready and waiting long before sunset. I occasionally stalk roe in the East Anglian breckland, where the deer emerge from the forest, usually at last light, to raid the neighbouring agricultural crops. In this situation they will often gather during the last half hour of light at a forward base on the edge of the forest, just far enough into cover so that they can feel safe but sufficiently close to the fields to detect anyone foolish enough to arrive late at his high seat. Although roe are not usually regarded as a herding species, when light levels are sufficiently low for them to feel safe, they will often emerge in substantial numbers. In the evening, the majority of shots are, in my experience, taken during the last half hour of legally shootable light.

Sometimes I have shot deer right up to the wire. One occasion which comes to mind was a roe doe taken at 6.10 p.m. at the end of February after a long evening's stalking. She had walked out of the adjoining forest in almost pitch darkness, but I just had enough light to see her silhouette against the grey bowl of the harvested sugar beet field in which she stood seventy yards away. On another occasion a professional stalker and I were trying to ambush some marauding red stags which had been emerging from a forestry plantation and causing crop damage on the estate. We had taken up position behind a crumbling dry stone wall and had waited since well before sunset. As night closed in, the deer had still not put in an appearance, so the stalker turned to me and whispered that we might as well pack up as it was getting too dark to shoot. However, judging that there were a few minutes of legal time left, I pointed out to him that even though it was hard to see with the naked eye, I still had a clear sight picture through my Schmidt & Bender 6 x 42 riflescope. 'OK,' he said, 'We'll give it five more minutes'. Shortly afterwards, two stags walked out of the wood some eighty yards away and, when my eyes readjusted after the muzzle flashes from my .308, I could see that both were lying dead on the grass. I reckon we must have been just about on closing time.

Weather conditions are an important consideration in deciding when to plan an outing. Indeed, they can be the deciding factor as to whether a stalker decides to go out at all. Heavy rain is a serious drawback. Hill stalkers don't worry about torrential rain, after all, it almost always seems to rain when you're hill stalking. The deer may be lying down but they are still out there on the hill and if you can spot them you can still stalk them. They are still there in the wood, of course, but the

● A successful shot at a February roe doe taken long after sunset, just before 'closing time'

problem is that they are tucked away in cover and you may not spot them unless you actually blunder into them. Few animals are willingly on the move in heavy rain. I have sometimes observed my own flock of sheep in such conditions, when it is evident that they prefer to be lying in the warm, dry patch of grass that they settled into before the rain started. Such observations usually take place when I have gone down to the meadow to check the flock upon my return from a wet, blank morning in the woods. Although the stalker is welcome to patrol the woods in torrential rain if he wishes to do so, I find that I rarely see very much under such conditions. Having said that, deer have to feed eventually. If wet weather continues over an extended period, especially in the hard, hungry months of late winter, then they will in due course be on their feet and visible to the stalker. More so the smaller species such as roe and muntjac which, with their smaller digestive systems, need to take on nutrition more regularly than larger animals.

Sun after rain, though, means that animals which have been lying up out of the weather will now have a chance to dry themselves off in the sun's warming rays and to fill their bellies. A bright sunny morning after a wet night is always a good time to go stalking and if overnight rain is predicted, then I try to check the internet forecast to see exactly what time the wet weather is expected to clear from my stalking ground. If, for example, frontal rain starts in the evening, with the sky being expected to clear just before dawn, then a trip to the woods is most certainly worthwhile. If the rain is expected to linger on into the morning, then it can be better to wait until last light before stalking.

Wind is an advantage, at least up to a point. A steady, serving breeze at least ensures that you know in which direction your scent will be carried and this has lots of advantages over a light, fluky wind which may send your scent drifting one way and then turn it in completely the opposite direction five minutes later. A reasonable breeze also creates a background of gentle noise which helps to mask any sound you make as you walk through a wood or along a ride and can enable you to stalk up quite close to a group of animals in a way that would perhaps be impossible on a still, crisp morning. Equally, though, you are less likely to hear deer when they are on the move in a wind, and although deer move quietly – far more quietly than humans – they do still make some sound. In a wind, you can sometimes find that a group of animals which you are stalking will disappear completely, almost as though the ground has swallowed them up.

In an ideal world, we would all have the flexibility to go stalking when we judge the weather conditions to be at their most favourable, but the practicalities of modern living often make this impossible, especially when stalking trips must be squeezed into a busy work schedule or the landowner, farmer or gamekeeper must be given lots of advance warning that you will be out in the woods. However, even if this is the case, a close eye on the weather forecast can help optimise the timing of your outings and at least reduce the number of blank days.

Although the law does not permit stalking at night, I always keep an eye on the phases of the moon. Of course deer are active during the hours of darkness as well as during the twilight of dawn and dusk: it only requires a drive around the edges of the woods at night with the car headlights on or with a hand-held spotlamp to see that. But though their night vision is excellent, they do require at least some light to feed at night. When there is sufficient moonlight, even the dim light of a moon which is filtered through a dense layer of cloud, deer will be active right throughout the night, and that can mean that they will already have done whatever feeding is required by the time legal shooting hours commence.

I know that I am not alone in having found that in some places, where shooting pressure coupled with the general intensity of human activity in the countryside has increased, deer – and especially fallow deer – have become almost completely nocturnal in their habits, especially during the winter months when the nights are long. This can make legal management very difficult indeed, for as the stalker enters the wood or takes up position prior to the last hour before sunrise, the deer will already have completed their foraging and will be finding somewhere to rest up. Furthermore, they will remain hidden until long after dark, only emerging when night has fallen once more. As the period between the beginning of November and the end of March is the only time during which females of most species may be shot, this can make the business of taking a realistic cull of females and young very difficult indeed.

However, once a month there is a short period when the nights are so dark that even deer that have become largely nocturnal will mostly be out and about during the twilight of dawn and dusk. This, of course, is around the time of the new moon, and I have found that early morning or late evening stalking trips taken at around that time can produce more success than those taken at other times of the month. I am lucky enough to stalk in countryside where there is very little artificial light and the countryside still is really dark at night. No doubt some deer that are closer to areas lit by street lights or industrial lighting will have learned to adapt to an almost completely nocturnal existence, but for me at least, the time of the new moon offers a further window of advantage which I can exploit.

10 Teamwork

ANY INDIVIDUAL STALKER faced with the responsibility of managing deer on a large farm or estate will be painfully aware that it is not always an easy task to ensure that an appropriate cull is taken which satisfies the requirements of the farmer or landowner. It is a tough enough task for the professional stalker who is able to allocate a substantial amount of time to deer management throughout the autumn and winter, but for the amateur, who must juggle with the demands of work and family, it is even more difficult to ensure that a reasonable job is done. Where the lone stalker has to dovetail with the requirements of other activities in the woods, such as game shooting or forestry operations, achieving a cull during the winter months when days are short and time is at a premium can be a tall order.

It is probably fair to say that deer stalkers tend in the most part to be loners who prefer their own company. Stalking is essentially a solitary activity which revolves around stealth, patience and great concentration. Its challenge is in the battle of wits between the individual hunter and a quarry which is both perfectly attuned to its natural environment and well able to look after itself. In the normal course of events, the deer stalker operates best when he is on his own, but there comes a time when he can achieve much more when he clubs together with a small group of others, working together with a common objective.

On his own, the stalker cannot hope always to be where the deer are, especially if the principal target is one of the herding species such as fallow deer, whose range may well be a good deal larger than the property which is being managed. However, bring together an experienced team of six or eight individuals onto a single estate and suddenly it becomes possible to man all the favourite places at one and the same time, thus greatly increasing the chances that at least someone is going to score success. More efficient use is made of stalker time and both skill and resources can be concentrated into a relatively small geographical area. When the formula is repeated, morning and evening, over a two or three day period, there is an opportunity for a much larger cull to be achieved than would be the case if the deer manager were stalking alone.

The basic ingredients for a successful team cull are fairly straightforward: an estate or stalking area which is large enough to be divided up into a series of distinct beats, irrespective of wind direction; a group of reliable and experienced rifles, or at least a relay of stalkers to plug the gaps over the duration of the planned cull; a sufficiency of suitable high seats and appropriate lardering facilities – these are the main essentials. If stalkers are going to be staying on site or nearby for a couple of days, then accommodation and catering may also need to be addressed. Where the organiser does not live locally, then a centrally located pub or, preferably, a holiday cottage which can be rented over a weekend makes the ideal base for operations.

Team culls are best scheduled for midwinter when the days are short, and when, with the morning stalk completed and a late breakfast polished off, there's not too much down time before the start of evening operations. Of course the winter months can be difficult where game shooting interests preclude access to the woods during the main part of the shooting season, but should that be the case, then February or even March is a good compromise.

Arranging a team cull is not difficult, but it necessitates careful planning. The first task must be to sit down with the farmer or landowner and agree timing and location, after which the basic plan should be discussed with anyone else directly involved with the running of the property such as the farm manager, forester and most especially the gamekeeper, who must be absolutely happy with a couple of days of deer culling taking place, possibly during the most important time in his calendar. Then a risk assessment should be undertaken by the organiser or deer manager. This can be carried out in conjunction with a map exercise which plots the optimum safe shooting positions and at the same time checks the location of footpaths, access areas, houses and farm buildings. Most of this information will of course be known to the deer manager anyway, but the concept of safe angles of fire may not be appreciated or understood by other farm or estate staff, whose cooperation will be essential to the success of the cull.

Organisation is vital and the most important element, once the support of the farm or estate has been assured, is to ensure that the right people are involved in the cull itself. In many cases these will be friends and colleagues of the deer manager: stalkers who are safe, trusted, reliable and competent, with their own appropriately conditioned certificates and rifles. If they have stalked the ground before as guests and if they have a basic knowledge of its geography then so much the better, but equally important if you want to put deer in the bag – and that surely must be the ultimate objective – is to have a core of experienced stalkers with the confidence to make the most of the opportunities which present themselves. Make arrangements well in advance of the proposed cull date, as many stalkers can find themselves very busy, especially during the months of February and March, after game shooting has finished.

Having drawn up a rota of who is going to be present on which days and who will occupy which beat or high seat at what time, you must give everyone details of when and where to meet, and those who do

● A photocopied map of the estate will help every stalker to become familiar with his beat

not know the ground well need to be given very clear directions on how to get there. Every stalker must also be made thoroughly familiar with the beat which he is being invited to hunt, if he does not know it already. A photocopied map of the estate is useful but an aerial photograph – easily accessible on the internet via Google Earth – can be even better, because it shows in great detail the exact features that the stalker will see on the ground. Mark on the map or photograph the locations of any high seats or fixed shooting positions and the boundaries of separate beats, while making sure that all potential danger areas such as roads, buildings and public rights of way are clearly indicated. If a visiting stalker is participating in the cull over two or more sessions, then offer him the opportunity to stalk a number of different beats if he would like to do so, recognising that he may perhaps prefer to get to know one individual patch really well over two or three days. From the visiting stalker's perspective, it is nice to be given a choice over where to go when visiting an estate over a long weekend, but as a guest myself I have sometimes enjoyed observing the movements of deer on day one on a particular beat and then, having stuck with that same beat over successive days, studied the lie of the land and used that reconnaissance to develop a killing strategy on day two or three.

Ensure that the agreed rendezvous time is sufficiently early as it may well be necessary for those stalkers who know the ground well to guide newcomers to their high seats in the pitch dark or to drive some distance across the farm or estate to drop off two or three rifles before taking up their own position. There is nothing worse than doing this when the grey glow of dawn is already showing in the east and potential shooting time is being eaten into. And to ensure that all appropriate parts of the property are fully accessible in the early hours of the morning when operations commence, don't forget to ask the farm manager to leave gates unlocked overnight or to issue drivers with keys that will allow them to gain access to important farm or estate tracks.

All stalkers should have a means of communication, either a mobile phone or a short wave radio, but for obvious reasons during the cull itself communications silence should be maintained – emergencies excepted – until a pre-arranged time when shooting will finish and rifles should be unloaded. In the evening this will normally be an hour after sunset, while in the morning it will be at an agreed time after sunrise. It is good practice to have an emergency stop procedure which is clearly understood by all participants.

In many cases, shooting from high seats will be the preferred strategy. A network of high seats distributed around an estate, covering every major glade, ride intersection or block of woodland, is a very effective way of getting a substantial number of rifles into a relatively small piece of countryside. Hopefully, wherever a deer is on the move within the shooting area, at least somebody should get a shot. Not everybody likes shooting from a high seat, but it has to be said that it is the best way of accommodating an appreciable number of rifles in a limited amount of space, and for those visitors who are unfamiliar with the local geography, a high seat really is the only sensible option, especially for the guest who perforce has to pitch up at 5.30 a.m. to an unknown estate and must be directed to his position before it starts getting light.

Permanent high seats may well be in position, but these can be augmented with portable seats erected on a temporary basis for the period of the cull. If additional seats need to be borrowed, then it is well worth contacting the regional office of the Deer Initiative (in England and Wales), for when there is a genuine job of work to be done, the DI may be prepared to offer portable high seats to an estate on loan over a weekend or a period of two or three days.

Decide first where any additional portable high seats should be sited, noting whether there are suitable trees against which to position lean-to seats and establishing which locations will require free-standing seats with leg kits. It is best to erect the seats a few days in advance if possible, in order to avoid excessive disturbance to the ground immediately before the cull date. A trailer behind a 4x4 vehicle or quad bike can be used to carry the portable seats and if you can get it close to the key locations, then a great deal of time can be saved. Naturally, when erecting high seats in temporary positions it is important to clear from lines of sight any undergrowth or overhanging branches which would obstruct the view from the seat or obscure an animal and thus prevent a shot from being taken, so remember to carry a bush saw or a pair of loppers with you. It is also an opportunity to trim back vegetation from around your permanent seats, a job which is easily neglected during the rest of the year.

The fact that most shooting will be from fixed positions need not, if the lie of the land and wind direction permit, prevent one or more stalkers from having the opportunity to stalk on foot, perhaps using a high seat as a base. Outlying woods which are separated from the main forest blocks may be quite suitable for an individual stalker to cover on foot, but it is of course essential that all stalkers are absolutely clear

● Many hands make light work of setting up temporary high seats

about the boundaries of the beats to which they have been allocated and that they do not stray beyond them.

Naturally, it is up to the deer manager to provide guidance on what may and what may not be shot. Are all species and sexes which are in season to be on the menu, or are particular classes of animal not to be culled? Does the gamekeeper require foxes to be shot? It is up to you to decide the shooting policy, based on your cull plan and the requirements of the estate.

Provision must be made for follow-up of lost or wounded animals. In the event that a deer is not found, it is up to the stalker concerned to establish the location of the strike and if necessary to call for an appropriately trained dog to locate the missing animal as soon as a halt to shooting has been called.

It is important to ensure that there are suitable arrangements in hand to deal with carcasses. The results of a successful muntjac or roe cull are easily popped in a tray in the back of a 4x4, but if larger species such as red, fallow and sika are being shot, then quad bikes, trailers or other suitable means of extracting carcasses will need to be arranged. On most estates where stalking takes place regularly there will probably already be a suitable larder, hopefully with a chiller unit in which to hang carcasses, but an organised cull can be expected to produce rather more carcasses than the larder would normally accommodate, so additional room may have to be found. If there is not an estate larder, then temporary facilities such as a mobile chiller trailer may have to be pressed into service in order that carcasses may be properly prepared for delivery to the game dealer at the conclusion of the cull. The Deer Initiative may be able to assist, and it is worth discussing your lardering arrangements with your DI regional officer.

Once morning stalking is over and any carcasses have been transferred to the larder, there may well be a period of 'down time' before the evening session begins, and with a group of willing stalkers to hand this offers a good opportunity to address one or more of the remoter, more undisturbed coverts by moving any deer which may be lying up within them towards static rifles. Moving deer in this way is not like the method of deer driving that is used in some parts of continental Europe and does not require a team of beaters; a single person, preferably wearing a high-visibility jacket and perhaps accompanied by a well-trained dog, walking slowly and quietly through a wood is quite enough to dislodge deer from where they are

● A full briefing for the team is essential before stalking commences

resting and to move them on to known deer paths or out across the surrounding fields. If the wood or cover is surrounded by a small number of experienced and well disciplined rifles, then this can be a very effective means of putting extra animals in the larder during the middle of the day when deer are not usually on the move.

When moving deer to static rifles it is absolutely essential that everyone understands where they are supposed to be, where the other shooters and walkers are and what their safe arcs of fire are should a deer emerge. If possible, rifles should be intervisible, but if not, then everyone should at least be in contact by radio or mobile phone. There is no need for the rifles to be posted close to the cover which is being walked, as would be the case with a driven game shoot. Indeed, if they are positioned well back, behind trees, hedges or other vantage points, then they will have more time to study any deer as the animals emerge, settle and hopefully move quietly away from the source of the disturbance. When selecting positions for static rifles, pay attention

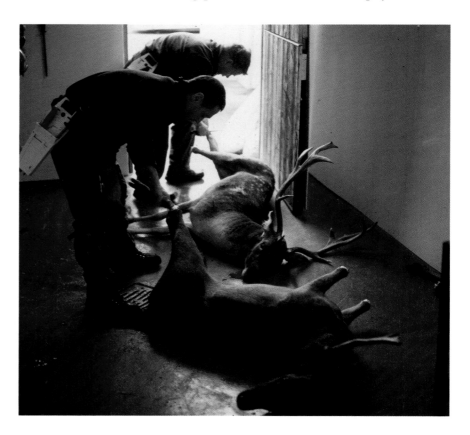

● All hands to the larder to deal with the results of a successful morning's work

both to the provision of safe shooting zones and good backstops, and also to any regular deer paths or favourite routes between the cover which is being walked and other nearby woods.

So much for the field logistics. Bringing together a group of stalkers over a weekend may well involve fixing up accommodation and catering, preferably on site or close to the shooting area. Unlike a day's game shooting, in which the Guns can conveniently turn up at 9.00 a.m. and depart at tea time or after a shoot dinner, two or three days of deer stalking will involve very early mornings, full afternoon and early evening sessions, and possibly a lot of work between times recovering carcasses and cleaning up in the larder. If the deer manager or organiser does not live close by, then a rented self-catering holiday cottage can work very well as a base for stalking operations. The unsocial hours, muddy gear, rifles and dogs may well rule out the local B&B so far as accommodation is concerned, but the local pub will certainly make a welcome venue for a convivial evening meal after stalking.

We always think of game shooting as a team activity, in which invitations are offered and others received in return, but the same can equally be true of deer stalking when you invite a small group of real friends, each of whom may have access to their own stalking ground, yet who themselves need a hand from time to time with achieving their cull and are not averse to swapping invitations. Furthermore, when the priority is to get high seats filled by competent rifles, there will be a welcome opportunity to offer an invitation to keen stalking friends who have no regular stalking of their own. Curiously in the context of the essentially lonely occupation of deer stalking, a team cull can be a really sociable event. That is especially the case when the holiday cottage is large enough to accommodate wives and girlfriends, some of whom may well be experienced and competent stalkers in their own right.

Although everyone has come primarily to do a job of work, the social side that is opened up by a team cull makes an operation of this sort hugely enjoyable. There is the sense of anticipation the evening before as maps are pored over, the weather forecast is checked and stalking beats are allocated. Or perhaps the rifles will gather before dawn in the estate yard, already in their boots and stalking kit, to receive their briefing and instructions. When, as it gets light and you are on patrol around the outermost extremities of the estate, there comes the sound of a shot from such and such a wood followed by another from a distant hedgerow, your spirits are lifted. 'That sounds as though Peter and Jeff have both had some luck,' you think to yourself, hoping that even if you score, there will be two extra deer in the bag at the end of

● When the priority is to get competent rifles on the ground, there is the opportunity to offer invitations to those with no regular stalking of their own

the morning which you could not possibly have accounted for by yourself. And perhaps there also rings out a shot from the high seat in which you placed a friend who, though experienced enough, has no regular stalking opportunity of his own. Just presenting him with the chance of a shot is hugely rewarding.

All is revealed when, at the agreed hour, mobile phones are switched on and messages are exchanged. Is there a call for assistance from a stalker who has a big beast to recover? Or does someone need the services of a dog to search for a missing animal?

Then, as the smell of frying bacon drifts temptingly from the cottage window, the team members arrive back for that most enjoyable of occasions, the stalking breakfast, late in the morning, with everyone gathered around the table, tucking into eggs, bacon, venison sausages and hopefully freshly shot roe or muntjac kidneys. Everyone will recount the successes of their morning's efforts – or tell those stalkers' tales of what might have been. More importantly, you very soon start to assess where deer have been seen and build up a picture of what their movements are, what fields they are feeding on, where they are lying up, and how best to intercept them that evening or the following day.

PART 3
AFTER
THE SHOT

11

The Stalker's Best Friend

IN THE DYING DAYS OF FEBRUARY, as the roe doe season was finally drawing to a close, I found myself late one Friday evening on the edge of a field in Norfolk's breckland. Judging by the fresh tracks leading out across the bare soil from the forest behind me, it was clear that a sizeable contingent of roe was in the habit of emerging at dusk to find what pickings they could amongst the recently harvested parsnip fields, and the ancient Scots pine under which I had concealed myself seemed as good a place as any in which to wait for them.

Darkness was closing in, however, and thus far there had been no sign of any roe. A deep, brooding silence had fallen across the forest, broken only by the twittering hoot of a tawny owl and the whirr of wings as a roding woodcock flitted across the ride that separated my clump of pines from the forest proper. There were barely ten minutes of legal shooting time left when I decided to call it a night and creep back along the ride to my car, but as I made my move, I spotted the unmistakable silhouette of a muntjac doe. She had stepped out onto the ride some sixty yards away and was broadside on to me, walking slowly across the open grass. Silently I opened my sticks to take a standing shot, and in a couple of seconds I had the deer comfortably in the reticle of my riflescope.

Squeezing the trigger, I was temporarily blinded by the orange flash from the muzzle of my rifle. There was no chance of observing the muntjac's reaction, but I was absolutely confident that the shot had been a good one and, as my eyes readjusted to the darkness, I paused before edging forwards into the open. Scanning the ride with my glasses I could see nothing, and as I approached the spot where the deer had been, there was not the slightest trace of the animal, alive or dead.

Fumbling in my pocket, I realised with a sinking heart that I had left my head torch at home, so there was not even any possibility of searching in detail for signs of a strike. However, I was not entirely without back-up. A phone call to my friend, who was stalking elsewhere on the estate, briefly outlined the problem, and a few minutes later I saw the lights of his 4 x 4 approaching along the track. In the back of the vehicle was his young flatcoat bitch, still a relative novice at the stalking game, but learning fast.

We came to the point where I had judged the deer to be standing when I fired and, like greased lightning, the young flatcoat shot into the dense forestry. It was the work of a few moments for her to find the deer, stone dead, some thirty yards inside the wood. The muntjac had run perhaps forty yards in total and despite the fact that my .308 bullet had passed through the top of her heart, I couldn't help thinking that without the assistance of a dog, this could well have been a lost deer.

In some European countries, it is actually illegal to go stalking unless you either have a dog with you or have access to one within a specific period of time after a shot has been taken. Here in Britain, we have long

● In some countries, such as here in Sweden, it is required that a dog such as this elkhound is available if necessary to follow-up wounded large game

regarded the use of a dog as optional, largely I suspect because of our Scottish tradition of open hill stalking. And yet for the woodland stalker, a well trained dog can make all the difference between a deer safely in the vehicle and a lost – or worse, wounded – deer out in the woods at night, a lengthy and difficult tracking process in prospect and a troubling and anxious time ahead for the stalker.

Most shotgun shooters would not dream of going shooting without a dog, whether their own, one belonging to a shooting companion or, at an organised shoot, a trained retriever handled by a dedicated picker-up. So why do we stalk without one? This question had not occurred to me until the first time I saw a dog find a lost deer of mine, a muntjac shot several years ago in not dissimilar circumstances to the ones I have just described. Again, the dog found the animal inside thirty seconds when I was fully expecting to be groping for hours on my hands and knees, looking for specks of blood in the dark on the forest floor. It was a revelation, but there was no reason why it should have been. After all, I have used Labradors to find lost wildfowl and gamebirds since I was thirteen years old and I have watched hounds hunt the line of a fox or hare across country since I was ten. The principle is exactly the same, indeed, it is probably fair to say that deer, which are a natural quarry of the wolf from which our domestic dogs are descended, are easier for a dog to follow than the birds which we commonly ask our gundogs to retrieve. Certainly the pack of beagles with which I used to hunt found the scent of deer at least as inviting as that of a hare, if not more so, causing much annoyance and a considerable amount of hard running for whippers-in such as myself.

There is what I regard as a belief among some woodland stalkers that if they take a dog out stalking with them it is there solely as a sort of safety net: a means of getting the stalker out of a hole when he makes a mistake, fires a badly placed shot and wounds a deer. Perhaps some stalkers do not have a dog with them because they do not accept that they are fallible.

But a dog is much more than an insurance policy against the moment when your shot goes awry and you wound an animal. Even a 'dead' animal will run hard between the time the bullet passes through its heart or lungs and the time that its legs cease to function and it crashes to the ground. Hard enough certainly to take it into the depths of thick and impenetrable cover. When faced with a missing muntjac, albeit a dead one, and a dense wall of bramble or thicket-stage conifers through which it is impossible even to walk, I have been very glad of my dog. And even if, as usual, there is no real work for her to do either because

● Your dog is much more than just an insurance policy: it is a companion in the field

the shot deer is both dead and plainly visible or we have had a blank visit, my bitch provides company when I am on my own in the fields and woods, and her delight and enjoyment when she takes from me the little pieces of heart or lung which I always offer her after the gralloch is a pleasure to watch in itself.

Blood scent or air scent?

Conventional wisdom holds that a stalking dog follows the scent of a blood trail. Training your dog to do this, by using a long cane with a line tied to the end, to which is attached a swab soaked in blood, is huge fun both for the dog and the owner, especially when the dog finds the 'deer' – usually a fresh deerskin concealed in a hedge – at the end of the trail and is given a tasty treat as a reward. Organisations such as BASC and the BDS now arrange regular 'Dogs for Deer' courses which, although neither designed for, nor capable of, training a stalking dog in a single day, do at least help to train the dogs' owners in the principles of blood trailing.

● Training a dog to follow a blood trail

1 Fill an open topped container with fresh deer blood

2 Using a long stick to keep your own scent away from the blood trail, dip an absorbent rag into the blood

3 Mark a trail with the blood-soaked rag

4 With the dog on a long check cord, encourage it to follow the trail

5 When it finds the fresh deer skin you have left at the end of the trail, give the dog lots of praise. Start with short, uncomplicated trails and slowly build up to more difficult ones

● Some breeds will follow the air scent of a deer in preference to the blood trail

● 'Here it is, dad!' A delighted Labrador with her find

Different breeds and even different individuals within those breeds perform in different ways, however, and while some dogs, such as the Teckels and Bavarian mountain hounds which are very popular amongst some stalkers, will indeed follow a blood scent with their noses glued to the ground, it is self-evident that others follow either the 'grass scent' of the herbage crushed by the fleeing animal, the molecules of body scent which cling to grass, twigs and leaves as the deer brushes past, the air scent of a shot deer or a mixture of all of these to find their quarry. I recall the first time I used my labrador bitch to find a fallow pricket which I had shot towards the end of the season in a crop of young wheat. Though clearly struck hard, the deer had run out of sight into the adjacent wood, which was already greening up with young spring growth. It was early in the morning; droplets of dew glistened from the tip of every cereal leaf and it was not difficult to see the track which the stricken animal had taken through the wheat field, brushing the moisture from the corn as it did so until it reached the grass margin which separated the wheat from the wood. While I searched hard for the blood trail to offer up precisely to my dog in the prescribed manner, the Labrador had other ideas. 'Don't fuss, dad,' she seemed to be saying, 'I can wind it from here!' So I let her get on with it. Hitting the line, head up like an old doghound in the Quorn country running a breast-high scent, she stormed into the wood and was fussing round the dead fallow within a few seconds. I was both amazed and delighted.

Since then, when I have asked my dog to find a deer, more often than not she will cast back and forth for the air scent, hunting through the cover in much the same way as she would if she were being asked to retrieve a dead pheasant or mallard.

Not every woodland stalking situation lends itself to using a dog. I am not convinced, for example, that it is always a good plan to have a dog

● Using a long check cord it is possible to train a dog to sit patiently under a high seat

sitting under your high seat for several hours, for however quiet the dog may be, it can still be winded by deer, or indeed other creatures approaching your position from the downwind side. On one occasion I recall watching a fox trotting along a ride towards where I was sitting in my high seat. I was following the animal in my scope, waiting for an appropriate moment to fire and so do the gamekeeper a service, when suddenly Charlie came downwind of the plume of scent from my dog, which was sitting quietly under my seat, concealed in the long grass. The fox didn't even pause long enough for me to squeeze the trigger and get a shot off – it bolted for dear life into the wood and I never saw it again. When I elect to sit in a high seat, I usually leave the dog in the back of my Land Rover, although if my plan is to sit for an hour or so until sunrise and then take a walk, then I will try to leave the vehicle at a convenient point so that I can pick the dog up later and let her stalk alongside me.

Having a dog with you when you are out stalking adds so much more to the day. Sometimes a dog can tell you that there are deer nearby long before you spot them, giving you invaluable early warning to slow down and prepare yourself for whatever might be about. It is really no different to the situation which is familiar to every roughshooter who works a gundog in front of him, when the dog's sudden change of demeanour is an instant indication of the need to bring the gun to the alert and place the thumb on the safety catch.

Curiosity killed the stag

However, I am of the opinion that there is yet another benefit to be gained from stalking with a dog, and that is that the sight of a dog actually seems to arouse the curiosity of deer. It was getting towards the end of April and I was making one last attempt to shoot a fallow buck before the season finally drew to a close. I had arrived at the farm by starlight and there was a sharp ground frost despite the steady westerly breeze. Getting to the corner of the wood around which I was planning to stalk, my dog and I turned into the wind. In front of us the sky was still dark and as the woodland edge curved away to our left we had the grey bulk of the trees behind us to provide cover against that rapidly brightening eastern horizon.

Below us a rough field of set-aside opened up into a big bowl, along the lip of which I walked carefully, stopping every three or four yards to study a landscape which was becoming lighter with every passing minute. As I carefully scanned the field, I noticed what appeared to be the two ears of a fallow doe poking up above the set-aside, and a few moments of observation confirmed that the deer was standing in the dead ground of the hollow. Being a female, it was out of season, but it was probably not alone. My dog was instructed quite firmly to sit and stay at the edge of the wood while I crawled forwards to investigate.

My belly crawl across the set-aside made me think more of stalking on the open hill in Scotland than woodland stalking in East Anglia, and when I reached the point where the ground dropped away in front of me, a further similarity to the Scottish hill became apparent: the deer were not fallow but red, part of the peripatetic herd that moved from wood to wood within the district and which had been eluding me all season. Occasionally I had found their tracks, while the keeper had once or twice spotted them on a shoot day but now, at last, here they were in front of me. There were six deer, four adult hinds and two youngsters, one of which was a knobber stag, all grazing quietly on the set-aside in the gloom of early morning, no doubt planning to spend the day lying up in the wood behind me. Clearly the hinds were out of season, but not so the young stag.

Cautiously I slid forward through the stubble and rough grass to a suitable tussock, just as I would creep through the Scottish heather in order to reach a firing point on the hill, and I took a good, long look with the glasses. Standing in the bowl of land beneath me, the deer offered a safe position for a prone shot from around 120 yards, so I picked out the young stag in my scope, pushed off the safety and the rifle barked out through the early morning air.

At the sound, five animals trotted forwards a few yards while the sixth stumbled and collapsed, but then a strange thing happened. Rather than disappearing at speed through the line of trees on the horizon, the deer turned towards me and stood stock still. Yes, I was downwind of them and they had not seen me approaching, but surely now that the potential danger was evident they ought to be away, instead of which they remained rooted to the spot as though they were magnetised. Nonplussed as to the reason for their odd behaviour I lay quite still and awaited developments, but the cause became apparent soon enough: I was not alone.

I am a firm believer in the old saying that if the dog misbehaves, then it is usually the fault of the owner, so I therefore accept full responsibility for the fact that my eager young bitch had found temptation too much to bear and, at the sound of the shot, had quit sitting at the edge of the wood and decided that it would be much more interesting to join me. So there was I, lying flat in the long grass with, prancing beside me, a very excited black Labrador bearing that crumple-faced expression of guilt that only a Labrador can wear.

My dog was what the deer were looking at, and those deer just couldn't contain their curiosity, for as I hissed at the dog to sit down, they trotted forwards towards us, coming up the rising ground a few yards before stopping, pausing and coming a few yards further. The seventy yard stand-off continued for what seemed like an age, though it was probably only three minutes or so that they hung around staring at the odd sight of a prostrate human being together with a black dog sitting bolt upright, goggle eyed.

Eventually they started to drift away, but they did not depart until I sat up and backed off, taking the dog with me. Even then the hinds, still curious, were in no haste to go. It was several minutes more before the coast was clear for me to deal with the stag.

● Deer are often curious yet unafraid when they see a dog

Since that day I have noticed on a number of occasions how deer are curious but unafraid of a dog, even when it has a deer stalker with it. Muntjac, which are usually the first to run for cover when they sense that something is not quite right, quite often stand stock still and look when they see a dog, giving me the opportunity to shoot. Perhaps they, and indeed other species of deer, are so used to seeing dog walkers in the countryside that the combination of human and canine holds no fear for them. But perhaps there are other instincts which kick in to prompt deer to stand and watch, rather than flee at the sight of a dog.

Decoymen traditionally used a small, foxy red dog to lure wildfowl into the long, curved, netted pipes which surrounded the old fashioned duck decoys which were introduced to Britain from Holland in the seventeenth century. Their craft exploited the fact that ducks, provided that they are safely afloat, will actually swim out of curiosity towards a fox which comes to the water's edge. In Scandinavia a spitz is used to hunt large woodland grouse such as capercaillie and black grouse. The little dog locates the bird and flushes it into a tree, whereupon the bird sits watching the dog as it stands under the tree and barks, enabling the hunter to approach unseen. In both these cases the quarry is instinctively familiar with the capabilities of its natural adversary, the fox or wolf, and while it is secure on the water or in the tree it knows that there is no need for it to expend unnecessary energy by taking flight. Instead it merely observes the predator closely to ensure that an adequate safety margin is maintained.

Could it be that deer are doing exactly the same thing when they see the stalker's dog? Knowing full well that a lone canine predator at a distance of seventy or eighty yards poses no immediate threat, is it their survival strategy to keep the predator under close observation in order that they can move away promptly at an appropriate speed should it become necessary to do so? I have now seen the stand-off between quarry and dog occur too often in a wide variety of quarry species to believe that it is merely coincidental and not something conditioned by the deep interplay of instinct between the hunter and the hunted.

The thought prompts a further consideration. Some stalkers deliberately select a dog with a colouration that blends naturally into the environment in which they are hunting. German wirehaired pointers, for example, are popular among stalkers not least because of their grey–brown broken coat. Indeed, I know of at least one stalker who likes to take his small, pale coloured dog with him, but who puts a camouflage coat on the animal so as to reduce the chance of its being spotted by deer. But, if the visibility of the stalker's dog – as opposed to that of the stalker himself – is an actual benefit to the hunting process, then do we actually need to conceal our dogs? I, and other stalkers I know, hunt with black dogs which are very obviously visible in the countryside, and although I have had many excellent days hunting with a variety of the continental HPR breeds and have a high regard for them, I do not think that their muted colouration is necessarily an essential requirement for the woodland stalker.

Tracking without a dog

Clearly, for some stalkers, keeping a dog is not a practical proposition, whether it be for family reasons, because of the nature of their employment or simply through lack of space at home. In this case, if a shot deer is not plainly visible, the stalker is faced with the painstaking business of following the visual trail. After waiting patiently for perhaps ten minutes and then marking clearly on the ground your position when you pulled the trigger, go directly to the point where you think the animal was standing when the shot was fired and check for signs of a strike. Plenty of bright, frothy blood and pins are the sign of a solid heart-and-lung shot, green stomach contents indicate a gut

● Telltale splashes of blood on the woodland floor. Lots of bright red blood usually means that the animal will be dead – and not far away

shot animal while bone fragments suggest a low shot which has shattered a leg.

The experienced stalker will already have gained an impression of the damage his bullet has done, both from the visible reaction of the animal which he has watched through the scope as the bullet hit its target and from the audible sound made by the strike. A solid thump followed by the classic lunge forward is a good sign of a heart-and-lung strike, though I occasionally find that muntjac and roe in particular will leap high into the air with a heart shot, especially a low one. Such a reaction always, in my experience, indicates a fatal shot, even if the animal runs off. A hollow thud followed by a hunched-up reaction is the unwelcome sign of a gut shot, while a bright sounding crack suggests broken bone and possibly a long and complicated follow-up.

It can be very difficult, walking across a large arable field crossed by several sets of tracks, to find the place where the target animal was struck, but there are other signs apart from hair and blood which one can look for. It is quite easy to see the heavy or scuffed slot marks made as the deer kicked or jumped when it was hit, and this is a good indicator even if there is no blood or hair. It also enables you to lock on to the set of footprints belonging to the animal you are looking to follow.

Blood trails may be sparse at first, but this need not necessarily be a cause for concern, for very often there will be much more copious amounts of blood at points where the animal has changed direction or gone through a hedge or over a fallen tree. If the strike is hard to find or inconclusive, then try to find the point at which the animal crossed a boundary, be it the edge of a field or a gap in a hedge, and try to pick the trail up from there.

It really is remarkable how an experienced tracker, using the evidence of his eyes alone, can follow a missing animal over the most unpromising ground. I recall hunting in the Karoo country close to the Orange River in South Africa's Northern Cape province with an African tracker called Guy. The two of us stalked up to a group of a dozen impala standing half-obscured in thorn scrub on a stony hillside

● Hunting in the Karoo country of South Africa's Northern Cape province. The African tracker on the left followed the trail of an impala for over three hours through the bush

and I took a shot at a big bull with the .300 Winchester magnum from a little more than 200 yards. As the animal went down, Guy turned to me with a big grin and shook my hand vigorously before running after the herd, which swiftly disappeared over the brow of the hill. By the time I had joined him he was searching the stony soil and dried up vegetation. We had both seen the animal collapse but there was no impala and not even any sign of blood at the place where he had gone down. It was some ten minutes and fifty yards later before Guy found the first blood splashes; there was more blood 100 yards after that, whereupon the trail descended into a dried-up river bed. Guy went on to follow a group of four impala, of which the stricken animal was one, for the next three hours across the most rugged bush country, intersected with ravines and koppies. He eventually found the impala, quite dead, and I have the trophy on my wall, a tribute to the most incredible demonstration of tracking I have ever been privileged to witness.

Such feats are the preserve of men who have been brought up to tracking in the bush from childhood in a country where dogs are not used for the simple reason that the game would be quite liable to kill them. Mere mortals such as myself require outside assistance to bolster our comparatively limited tracking ability when the trail goes cold. If a dog is not available, then other options exist such as infra-red detectors and blood revealing reagents, both of which I have tried with some success. The second of these can only be used after dark, but that of course is the time when help is most needed. A couple of blood-revealing chemical tablets diluted in a 500 ml handispray filled with water will make blood splashes quite literally glow in the dark like patches of bright blue phosphorescence, and I once tracked a muntjac road accident victim at night across a field and found it using this product. Even so, I am firmly convinced that it is far better to have a dog, even a dog of modest training and ability, than to have no dog at all. Furthermore, a dog is much better company than a handispray during the course of a morning's stalking in the countryside.

12 A Moving Experience

IT IS OFTEN SAID that pulling the trigger is the easy part of deer stalking and that the difficult bit is what comes afterwards. How true those words are, as you will no doubt agree when at around 4 p.m. you are finally hosing down the larder after having risen several hours before dawn, stalked, shot and gralloched two or three large beasts, dragged them single-handedly out of the wood, loaded them, again by yourself, into your vehicle, driven home and prepared them for the chiller.

After one or two such experiences there might even come a time when, with a red deer or a big fallow buck in your sights, you elect not to take the shot simply because it would be impractical to get the carcass back to the larder. Even though the animal is in season and a legitimate target, it can sometimes be that the place where it is standing is completely inaccessible to the vehicle which you have available, you are stalking alone and there is nobody whom you can call on to help drag the carcass to a more convenient spot. Or perhaps you have shot sufficient large animals to make the workload of taking a further one unacceptable. To put another animal on the ground would be the straw which broke the camel's back and unfortunately you would be the camel.

Usually decisions like this will be faced when you are on your own, a long way from any assistance, on difficult terrain which is perhaps thickly wooded, boggy or steeply sloping. In these circumstances it is wise to consider the practicality of carcass extraction before you set out, and mentally impose a set of limits upon your actions. One of the pieces of ground where I shoot regularly, for example, has steep hills and a heavy clay soil which, after a few weeks of wet weather, becomes impossible for my Land Rover to access, even with the all-terrain tyres

● Recovery of big animals can require team effort. Seven hunters are needed to drag this bull moose through the Swedish forest to where it can be reached with a vehicle

which I always use between October and April. Nor, on that particular piece of ground, is it feasible to call up a tractor either to haul out a deer or a mudbound or grounded vehicle. In the early autumn, or even in the depths of a hard freeze, it might be a simple job to access a carcass. But in a wet winter, when the land is saturated and the water

is lying deep in the furrows, I will think very carefully before pulling the trigger at the unexpected appearance of a big red deer. If a muntjac or roe stands before me, then carrying the carcass back to the vehicle will present no difficulty, but where a larger species is involved, then I will consider first whether recovery is a practical proposition.

If there are willing volunteers available, such as during a team cull, the situation will be completely different. Many hands make light work and in Sweden, where an adult moose will weigh three or four times the weight of one of our big forest stags, hunting is a cooperative venture. A rope with a series of snap rings is attached to the dead moose, whereupon each member of a team of hunters clips his own rope onto one of the rings and in this way six or eight men can pull a big animal through the most uncompromising rocky or forested terrain to a place which is accessible to a quad bike and trailer. The hunters there are fully prepared for the recovery of huge animals from very remote terrain, just as the Scottish deer forest is equipped with quad bikes, Argocats or ponies which are capable of bringing a big stag down from the hill. It is simply a matter of thinking in advance about the equipment and the assistance at your disposal, plus the terrain and the ground conditions.

The gralloch

Where wild deer are concerned, the gralloch is almost always undertaken at the place where the deer has been shot. In the context of woodland deer, this usually involves the removal of the entire digestive tract (the 'green offal') and the thoracic contents including the heart, lungs and windpipe (the 'pluck'), though highland stalkers, and some lowland ones too, prefer to leave the diaphragm intact and the thoracic contents in place until the carcass reaches the larder. This latter course of action certainly reduces the chances of contamination if the animal is to be dragged any distance, but equally, removal of the entire gralloch in the field will reduce the weight of the carcass if it is to be dragged or carried. Both options are acceptable in the right circumstances and you must decide for yourself which is more appropriate, remembering that if you are planning to remove the pluck back in the larder, then the carcass must be bled as soon as possible after death.

Personally, I prefer to undertake the full gralloch in the field, wherever possible suspending the carcass from the branch of a convenient tree. In the case of roe and muntjac, I do this by using the 9 feet (3m) of thin rope which I always carry in the pocket of my stalking jacket especially for this purpose. Knot the rope around one of the hind legs by way of a hole pierced through the hock and you can hoist the carcass over a branch, twisting the rope a couple of times around the branch to lock it in place before pushing the other end of the rope through the hock of the other hind leg and tying it off so that the animal is suspended, hind legs apart, at a comfortable working height.

For larger species I have a lightweight hook and pulley kit which comes in two parts and which is perfect for use in the field. First there is a gambrel comprising a webbing strap linked to three stout hooks. A tubular steel spreading bar is inserted between the bottom two hooks, and because this is made in detachable sections, it can be shortened or lengthened according to the species concerned. Once the gambrel has been inserted through the hocks of an animal, it is hooked to the lower of a pair of pulleys and the whole carcass can then be raised easily by hauling on the webbing strap with which the kit is supplied, the top

● With small deer like this muntjac, hoist the carcass over a branch so that the animal is suspended, hind legs apart, at a comfortable working height

● Suspending the animal makes it easy to cut around the anus and free the rectum

pulley having first been suspended from a convenient branch. Make sure that the strap is tied off securely and you can work on the deer with ease, and without the need for the carcass ever to come in contact with the ground once it has been opened. This simple block and tackle device, which is capable of lifting 800 lbs (360 kg) if ever called upon to do so, weighs only 1 lb 6 oz (625 g) so it could easily be carried in a rucksack, though I usually keep mine in the back of the Land Rover together with a couple of spare ropes. I have used it to lift large forest red stags, though of course if you intend doing so, it is essential to have a stout overhanging branch which is sufficiently strong to lift the deer from. After the gralloch has been completed, it is a simple job to back a vehicle underneath the suspended carcass and lower it directly into a trailer or pick-up.

Where there is no option but for a large animal to be gralloched on the ground, then there is a trick I learned from a Swedish moose hunter which will make it much easier to keep the hind legs apart while

● The gralloch is completed quickly and easily

● With the help of a lightweight hook and pulley kit, it is a simple matter to suspend a larger carcass from a tree for gralloching

● When gralloching a large animal on the ground, tie one of the hind legs to a tree to keep the legs apart when opening up the abdomen

opening up the abdomen. My friend keeps a length of nylon line in his pocket. One end of the line is attached to the uppermost hind leg of a felled moose while the other is hitched around a nearby tree. Pull on the free end of the line to lift the leg and then tie the line off to keep the leg raised while you are working on the carcass.

It should go without saying that the gralloch should be kept as clean as possible, avoiding rupture of the digestive tract, though this cannot always be avoided if the shot has been less than perfect. However, the cleaner, the more careful and the more precise your gralloching operation is, the easier it will be to check over the mesenteric lymph glands as part of your overall inspection of the animal's health, and thus ensure its fitness to enter the food chain. It has to be said that to find an unhealthy deer is a rarity. I have once shot a roe doe with liver fluke, which was clearly indicated by the blotchy surface of the liver, but apart from that one animal the only deviations from 100 per cent fitness which I have encountered have been caused by injury such as fractures, fights with other deer or, sadly, shotgun wounds. That said, the fact that our wild deer are by and large remarkably healthy is no reason to skimp on the examination which is required before a carcass can be sent to the dealer.

Disposing of the gralloch can be a sensitive matter. For the highland stalker it is easy: he leaves it out on the hill for the ravens and the eagles. In the lowlands it is generally best to tidy it away, simply because there tend to be more people out and about in the countryside, some of whom might well find the sight of a gralloch distasteful. Burying is the usual option, and I always carry a folding entrenching tool on my belt with which to dig a hole. Good practice indicates that gralloch should not be buried where it might contaminate water courses, but bearing in mind this consideration I usually try to make my life as easy as possible by digging in an existing depression, such as the pit formed under the detached root ball of a fallen tree, especially on a property where the soil is heavy and the digging is difficult. Remember to cut or slash the stomach, rumen and large intestine before backfilling the hole. I usually scatter dead leaves over the burial site, making it as invisible as possible, to human eyes at least, though one has to accept that buried gralloch is easily discovered by hungry foxes and badgers.

● Dig a hole to bury the gralloch

● Scattering a few dead leaves will help to conceal the burial site

Naturally the landowner has every right to dictate how grallochs should be disposed of, and it is good policy to discuss this issue with him before starting to stalk in a new area. While the occasional gralloch dug up and eaten by scavenging foxes will not usually cause offence, the discovery of scattered heads and feet which have been disinterred by the local wildlife can cause distress to members of the public. They can also, by the way, spark false alarms of suspected deer poaching. I do not bury heads or feet. Instead, I dispose of them at the larder.

Intriguingly, environmental considerations can lead to two completely divergent schools of thought so far as disposal of deer remains is concerned. In one situation that I know of where deer stalking takes place in a nature reserve which is open to the public, the rule is that grallochs must be removed from the site altogether. Yet in the New Forest, road casualty deer are simply lifted from the road, taken into the woods and left to decompose naturally or be eaten by predators and scavengers. It is felt, with some justification, that the deer have come from the forest and that it is ultimately to the forest that they should be returned by the cycle of nature. This is a philosophy with which I find great sympathy.

A regular routine is most important when gralloching deer, especially when doing so in the middle of a wood at night by the light of a head torch, otherwise you are liable to leave your stalking gear distributed all over the countryside. It really is so easy to put things down, knives especially, and then to forget where you have put them. When the woodland floor is covered in dead leaves and undergrowth this can quickly result in some expensive piece of kit getting lost. First unload your rifle, and if it has a detachable magazine then remove the magazine and replace in it the round which you have removed from the chamber. I always put my magazine in the same pocket of my jacket and then stand the rifle against a tree, my stalking sticks beside it. Gloves can easily go missing. I put mine, plus my face mask and binoculars, in my hat and put this on top of my jacket which of course I remove before starting work. My watch goes in the left hand pocket of my breeks. I do not suggest that everyone must follow this routine, but do at least follow some routine, whatever it may be, or you'll risk losing a favourite gadget or accessory. And although it can seem an unnecessary burden, if there is a journey to make back to the vehicle on foot, then I always put my gear back on after the gralloch is finished. On goes the jacket and hat, on goes the belt with my folding spade and sheath knife. Round my neck go the binoculars, just as they do when I get kitted up on starting the stalk. That way, everything gets accounted for, or at least it should do.

Moving and handling carcasses

After gralloching, it is time to get your deer out of the wood. Muntjac and roe are straightforward for the lone stalker to extract by himself. Some stalkers use a roe sack, suitably lined with a waterproof liner that can be cleaned of blood after use, to carry a carcass out on the shoulders. For muntjac, I usually make use of my 9-foot rope by tying the back legs together at the hocks, tying the front legs together at the knees and looping the rope three or four times between the two pairs of legs to make a handle. An alternative option is to find a suitable branch – a stout hazel rod is ideal – and slip it between the two pairs of tied legs. If you are stalking with a companion, then you can carry the animal out of the wood as you might a sedan chair. One of my muntjac shooting friends uses a carrying device, rather like a game carrier, made from a broad leather strap. Both ends of the strap are divided lengthwise for about 10 inches (25 cm) and four brass rings are attached. To carry a muntjac, he loops each leg into a noose made by pushing an end of the strap through one of the brass rings, just as you might if you were to carry a pheasant by the neck with a game carrier. Then he simply places the strap over his shoulder.

● It is easy to carry a muntjac by tying the back legs together, tying the front legs together and looping the rope between the two pairs of legs to make a handle

Larger deer usually need to be dragged, unless you have been so lucky as to be able to shoot them at a spot to which you can gain access with your vehicle. Dragging can be fairly straightforward when the way is downhill and the surface is grass, heather or other short vegetation. Unfortunately this is rarely the case with low ground deer, which invariably have to be pulled out of thick woodland or across flat, heavy, wet fields. It is hard work even for two people. For the lone stalker it can be backbreaking stuff. A long drag can also result in a carcass becoming caked in mud or stripped of hair along its flank, in either case making it less presentable to the game dealer even if it has not actually been contaminated with soil or debris. At the very least, drag the carcass from the front end, so that the direction of movement does not pull against the coat. Preferably, use a drag bag. This accessory may be bought from a stalking supplies retailer but it is quite easy to make with a piece of heavy gauge plastic-coated canvas sheeting, a series of large brass eyelets and a suitable length of nylon or polypropylene rope. Simply lay the canvas sheet next to the carcass, roll the animal onto it and lace the drag bag up

● This fallow pricket is fully gralloched and ready for dragging out of the wood. Note that the liver and kidneys will be removed back at the larder

● This cull buck has been dragged back to the vehicle in a drag bag

● If you can get a 4x4 vehicle close to where you have shot the animal, then carcass recovery is much easier

● Loading carcasses into a sled keeps the centre of gravity of a laden quad bike close to the ground

with the rope. The plastic surface of the drag bag greatly reduces friction with the ground, making the drag an easier one, while also protecting the carcass from contamination. If you are shooting in woodland to which the public has access, this strategy also avoids unsightly blood trails between the site of the gralloch and the vehicular access point which might cause offence to visitors. A slightly more sturdy variation on the dragging theme is the sled, into which larger animals may be manhandled, the sled then being towed behind a quad bike. Using a sled is a much safer option than loading the carcass directly onto the bike itself, especially for the lone stalker, because it reduces the lifting and handling issues associated with heavier carcasses and it also ensures that the centre of gravity of the laden quad bike remains low to the ground.

Actually getting the deer into a vehicle is the next consideration. Again, it is easy with small deer and difficult with big ones. It is good practice to use a plastic carcass tray or some other suitably sized washable plastic container to put a muntjac- or roe-sized carcass in, thereby keeping all blood, gore and other grime from soiling the vehicle while also ensuring that the carcass itself is not contaminated. There are even fully insulated carcass boxes available in up to small fallow size which can be lined with pre-frozen gel packs, thereby helping to get a carcass down to suitable storage temperature and keep it cool,

● Small deer can be loaded easily into a carcass tray in the back of the vehicle

● Use of an all-terrain vehicle greatly reduces the need to drag or manhandle carcasses

even during the course of a long journey. Carrying large carcasses in the back of a vehicle ideally means purchasing a plastic, glassfibre or even stainless steel tray or liner which can be washed down after use, unless you are happy to use a hose in the back of your pickup or 4x4. An alternative is to get hold of a large plastic sheet or tarpaulin with which to line the back of the vehicle before loading in the deer. It is more difficult to clean than a rigid liner, but a far more attractive proposition than trying to scrub deer blood from the upholstery of your new Range Rover, especially deer blood which has ripened over a few hours of hot autumnal sunshine.

To lift, singlehandedly, a large red deer into a vehicle with a high tailgate, such as a Land Rover, is a very tough job indeed. For many years I drove a Citroen estate car in which it was possible to lower the suspension, thus dropping the tailgate down almost to ground level.

That car was great for loading heavy deer – provided the ground was hard enough to get the vehicle onto it in the first place. However, lifting very heavy carcasses is definitely not to be recommended if you are singlehanded and can indeed cause serious injury, though a big deer can be reduced in weight to some extent by removing the head and lower legs. There are, however, a couple of options. One is to fit a winch behind the cab of a pick-up or 4x4 and keep a couple of stout boards in the load compartment to use as a ramp. It then becomes an easy job to winch the animal into the load space. Alternatively you can buy a vehicle-mounted gantry hoist which will raise the carcass to pick-up height and then lower it into the back of an open-topped vehicle. However, a trailer is probably a more flexible option as it will certainly accommodate more carcasses than the average 4x4 pick-up. A general purpose galvanised road trailer with an 8 x 4 ft bed and a ramped tailgate works very well indeed, especially if it has a winch attached to it. However, one designer has even developed a road-legal trailer which will take both your carcasses and your quad bike at one and the

● This trailer will carry both carcasses and a quad bike. The carcasses are loaded into the trailer bed and the bike is parked on the ramped tracks

same time. The carcasses are loaded into the trailer bed and protected by an impervious cover that is drawn over them. Then two ramped tracks are folded down over the top of the trailer and hey presto, you can park your quad on top.

Trouble free carcass handling and extraction relies on being geared up for the terrain and the expected species. In a situation where nothing larger than roe are anticipated, there is little more that is required than a groundsheet or a carcass tray in the back of your 4x4 – or even your family saloon. But on ground where you know from experience that you can expect to shoot big, heavy deer, then prior thought and preparation is required, together with some investment in appropriate lifting and handling equipment.

13
The Stalker's Larder

IT REALLY IS QUITE REMARKABLE what an impact the 2006 Food Hygiene Regulations have had on the entire shooting industry. By interpreting into British statute a series of European Union regulations on food hygiene and traceability, this new set of laws has significantly changed the procedures by which wild game and venison are taken into the food chain, stored, prepared and marketed. Despite the inherently conservative nature of those involved in shooting and stalking, sporting estates have been quick to react to the changes and there cannot be many employed gamekeepers and professional stalkers who have not by now become 'trained hunters', qualified to inspect carcasses and approve them for acceptance by the dealer.

The same may be said for independent deer managers and recreational stalkers. Anyone now sitting the Deer Stalking Certificate Level 1 assessment will, as a matter of routine, receive the instruction which is required for the large game element of the 'trained hunter' qualification, while those who took their assessment prior to the introduction of the 2006 Regulations have had the opportunity to update their knowledge and become trained hunters for the purpose of placing venison into the human food chain.

There can be no question about it: any person who is stalking or managing deer in his own right, that is to say without the guidance of a professional stalker, should nowadays seek to attain trained hunter status. Without it he cannot easily sell carcasses to a game dealer – now termed an Approved Game Handling Establishment (AGHE) – and he is thus effectively limited to preparing that which he shoots for consumption by himself, his family and friends. Admittedly, this is all that many recreational stalkers wish to do, but for the serious manager of deer, the inability to sell carcasses on to the dealer is a major stumbling block, especially where the larger species such as fallow and red deer are concerned, because their potential size makes preparation for consumption on a domestic scale problematic, if not impossible. Most game dealers, on the other hand, have invested very substantial sums of money in developing facilities for the preparation and butchering of such animals to a high standard, and while the average stalker might consider skinning and cutting the occasional larger carcass for the freezer, it is probably not something which he would wish to contemplate on a regular basis.

But it is not only game dealers who have upgraded their premises. Only two years after the introduction of the new Regulations, research by the Countryside Alliance found that over half of all sporting estates had upgraded their game storage facilities and that two thirds had installed a chiller capable of keeping game or venison at the temperature appropriate for storage prior to preparation or onward sale.

● State of the art in 1890, but times have moved on for this game larder

Until quite recently, probably the majority of sporting estates have relied upon game larders, often a century or more old, comprising little more than a fly-proof outbuilding fitted with hanging rails for deer carcasses or hooks for feathered game, with hopefully a running water supply and a place for the gamekeeper or stalker to wash his hands. No doubt such facilities were 'state of the art' in 1890, and in most cases they have served their purpose well for many years, probably without any major mishap.

I still meet professional estate stalkers without access to proper chilled storage, but by and large the day of such primitive facilities is now over. Modern larders range from state-of-the-art units costing tens of thousands of pounds down to quite modest facilities in which the original building has been quickly and simply brought up to standard through the introduction of a chiller. Given that the only proper alternative, during the warmer months of the year at least, is to deliver carcasses directly to the dealer's cold room from the wood or field in which they have been shot, the construction of at least a basic lardering facility and cold store is something which the serious stalker should think about in some detail.

● A redundant dairy building made the perfect starting point for conversion into this deer larder

A wide variety of different structures can be considered for conversion to a working deer larder. While not all of us are lucky enough to own a farm, the majority of properties where deer stalking takes place will contain farm or estate buildings, some of which may be underused and have space for the preparation and storage of deer carcasses shot on the premises. Former livestock farms are a good hunting ground for disused dairy buildings which will almost certainly have sound concrete floors laid to fall, ample drainage and possibly even mains water. If you do not own a suitable building yourself, then a word with the farmer or landowner from whom you obtain your stalking rights may pay dividends. Indeed, your investment in improving his buildings could conceivably help to secure your stalking long into the future. But if no farm or estate buildings are available, then there are other options. Most houses in the countryside have at least some form of outbuilding and even a wooden garden shed can be turned into a workmanlike larder which is quite sufficient to prepare a carcass to an acceptable standard.

Remember that the Food Hygiene Regulations apply to the operation of game larders and that where a larder is used to store unskinned carcasses or for the basic dressing of carcasses for onward transport to an AGHE, then it is regarded as part of a food business and must be registered with the local authority.

When planning a deer larder there are a number of essentials to consider. The roof must be sufficiently high to allow a working height of around two metres from the rail, hook or hanging point to the floor. If red deer are anticipated, then even more height may be needed, and remember that a high ceiling or roof space will enable air to circulate. Above the working area there will need to be one or more suitable beams or structural members – steel or timber – which are capable of safely supporting the largest carcass you expect to shoot. If no such beam exists, then consider installing a joist to which your hanging rail or hooks can be fixed.

Hygiene is of prime importance and thus a well-drained concrete floor which can be washed down is ideal. If desired, this can be sealed with a polyurethane floor paint or even an epoxy resin coating. Consider also the wall surfaces. Purpose-built food preparation buildings will often be clad with plastic-coated sheeting, but a good cement render is very acceptable when you are converting an existing building on a budget, especially when it is painted with a couple of coats of exterior quality masonry paint. Ideally your proposed larder should have its own mains water supply and hand washing facilities, but a hose from a nearby tap can at least be a perfectly adequate way of washing the floor and walls. Access to mains electricity for lighting and power is essential.

Consider the need for space to accommodate lardering equipment, a table and perhaps a freezer, but most importantly allow sufficient space for a chiller, for whether a carcass is destined for the dealer or for storage on your own premises, the likelihood is that it will need to be chilled. The law does not actually require the installation of a chiller in so many words and during the coldest months, especially in Scotland and northern England, it might be possible to achieve appropriate storage temperatures in ambient air for considerable periods. However, Food Standards Agency guidance states that you should 'take account of the requirement for chilling to start within a reasonable period of time after killing, achieving a temperature throughout the meat of 7°C for large wild game'. In most cases, and certainly during the summer or autumn months in the south of England, this will necessitate artificial refrigeration.

Having your own chilled storage buys time. It means that, from the moment you are gralloching a shot beast in the field and loading it into the vehicle or onto a trailer on a warm autumn morning with the heat of the day ahead, you are not fretting about how quickly it can be driven to the game dealer's premises, always assuming those premises are open and accepting carcasses on the day you are stalking. It means that, instead of having to chase your tail throughout the winter, constantly having to keep an eye on the ambient temperature and being obliged to skin and prepare carcasses within a short time of shooting them, you can gather a batch of animals together and then dress them all at a time which is convenient to you.

The route which many larger sporting estates have taken is to develop a cold room by lining an existing building with insulated panels and introducing cold air from an externally mounted chiller unit. For a sporting estate with a significant stalking operation and probably a game shoot as well, the cost of lining existing walls with insulating panels is not exorbitant. A rough estimate may be made by assessing the cubic capacity of the room to be insulated: allow around £200 per cubic metre of larder space for larders of between 10 m³ and 20 m³, £140 per cubic metre for those between 20 m³ and 40 m³, and £100 per cubic metre for those in excess of 40 m³. As to the refrigeration equipment itself, a very competitive alternative to conventional refrigeration equipment is a 'monobloc' unit, a complete one-piece refrigeration unit which is inserted through a panel in the cold room

● This redundant farm building has been converted into a first class larder and preparation room

and which requires no pipework or complicated electric engineering. Designed primarily for the catering market, where the object is to maintain at low temperature goods coming into store which are already chilled, monobloc units are not so effective at quickly reducing warm carcasses down to the required holding temperature, and it is argued by conventional refrigeration experts that they may tend to dry out the carcasses – which could be a disadvantage when the estate is being paid by carcass weight. However, they are cheap to install and a small monobloc unit costing around £1,500 will effectively chill a larder with a capacity of around 22 m³.

Alternatively, several of the leading suppliers of refrigeration equipment to the farm and estate market now offer a fully bespoke service by which they will design and install a custom-built larder which is exactly tailored to the user's requirements, including all the chilling and handling equipment, plus the preparation area. Before working up a design, the supplier will ask the estate manager to specify how many carcasses of what species they are expecting to take in and store over what period, so some careful thought needs to be given to deciding upon these parameters, while perhaps some allowance might be made to accommodate growth in the future.

This sort of package will be out of the price bracket of most recreational stalkers and private deer managers, even quite active ones,

● Mechanical lifting and handling equipment ensures that carcasses can be moved straight from the delivery vehicle through this custom-made estate larder

but even for them there is now a wide range of small static self-contained chiller units on the market which require nothing more than a firm, level concrete base inside an existing building or under some other appropriate weatherproof structure, plus a mains electricity supply. Several of these are delivered flat-packed for self assembly, thus keeping costs down whilst at the same time ensuring that the unit can be transported in pieces through narrow doors and difficult access routes. Size will be dictated by the number and species of the carcasses you wish to store, while the heat loading and thus the capacity of the refrigeration unit will depend on the number of carcasses which have to be brought down to temperature at any one time. Always remember, when considering the installation of a self-contained chiller in an existing building, that sufficient space must be allowed around the chiller unit for ventilation and heat dispersal. The basic cost of a static self-contained chiller with floor dimensions of 1.4 m x 1.8 m will be

● This Landig fridge will comfortably take two fallow carcasses or six muntjac

around £2,400 while a small self-assembly cold store capable of holding four roe or two fallow and measuring 1 m x 1 m can be had for around £2,000 plus VAT.

Another option is a game fridge, which is essentially a large, tall refrigerator capable of holding a number of deer carcasses. These are popular in Germany and are available in several sizes, right up to large units that will take big red deer carcasses. Being German, they are also superbly engineered, thus avoiding any of the potential problems associated with self-assembly chiller units. When developing my own larder from a former farm building, this was the route I chose, and my own Landig fridge comfortably takes a couple of large fallow carcasses or half a dozen muntjac. It has its own integral twin hanging rails and a tough plastic interior which is incredibly easy to keep clean. The stainless steel drip tray which I bought as an additional accessory may be removed for washing. The price was under £1,500, which, when you think about it, compares favourably with a top-of-the range riflescope. My only nervous moment was when I found that the fridge, when it arrived all neatly packed on a pallet, was just a quarter of an inch too wide to get through the door of my new larder. To get it inside I had to remove the larder door and doorstops.

When planning a larder it is important to consider how carcasses are to be handled within the preparation area, and the logistics of this will vary greatly between the different species. A stalker who is shooting principally muntjac or roe will be able to lift and handle individual carcasses without too much difficulty, however, this is not necessarily the case when fallow, sika or red deer are involved. Given that the average age of a BASC recreational stalker is 48, that of a professional stalker is 51 and rising, and that 70 per cent of BDS stalkers are over the age of 45, the matter of moving and handling large carcasses bears some serious consideration.

When developing my own larder I made sure that I installed an electric winch, for I was determined to avoid future hernias with those

● The Güde GSZ electric winch makes short work of lifting heavy carcasses

big fallow bucks. In the past I have used reduction geared chain lifting tackle for really big beasts, but although such equipment may be good for lifting engines out of tractors, draping a moving chain around a deer carcass as you are lifting it is not exactly ideal. My Güde GSZ electric winch is capable of lifting up to 125 kg and if greater capacity than this should ever be required, the unit is supplied with a guide sheave which enables me to double up the cable, thus allowing loads of up to 250 kg to be lifted. It is powered off a conventional domestic supply and is operated by means of a chunky yellow handset which contains a simple rocker switch to raise or lower the load. The handset also has a large red button which immediately stops the motor in an emergency, and this button can be locked by turning it clockwise a quarter turn. A further safety feature is the switching level ring, which stops the motor when the lifting hook is in the fully raised position, thus preventing any risk of overstraining the cable. With a retail price of just £155, I reckon that the winch represents money well spent.

When installing a winch there are two important considerations to bear in mind. First it must be secured to a structural beam which is capable of taking the service load at which the unit is designed to operate, plus a margin for safety, and second it must be fixed at a height which enables a carcass to be raised above the hook onto which it is being delivered. Careful planning with a tape measure is required in

● A ceiling track and roller system is fitted inside this cold room

order to avoid mistakes which are embarrassing, time consuming, costly or all three.

The ideal arrangement when working with heavy carcasses is to have a ceiling track and roller system which extends from the intake point right through to the cold store itself. This enables the operator to winch a carcass out of the trailer or vehicle in which it is delivered to the larder, then to move the carcass to the work area for preparation and, if it has not been completed in the field, gralloching. The carcass may then be moved directly into cold storage, if it is to be held in its skin; or otherwise it can be skinned and chilled. At each stage of the process it is a simple matter of pushing the suspended carcass onto the correct track, and a large number of animals may be manoeuvred and handled with great ease. Some systems are manufactured from food grade aluminium and because of their light weight they can be adapted to most larders, though they may only have a safe working limit of around 350 kg per metre length. More robust systems, manufactured from galvanised steel, are suited to use with the larger species. However, an overhead rail system is expensive to install and is unlikely to be cost-effective for the home stalker. Much more appropriate is a single rail and hook system, which can either be bought from a company which supplies cold store accessories or made up by a local blacksmith or agricultural engineer at a fraction of the price.

Being lucky enough to have a set of hanging rails and wrought iron hooks salvaged from a defunct butchers shop, all I needed for my own larder were the brackets required to suspend my rail beneath the large structural timber joist that I had cut into the blockwork of the building I had converted. Two brackets, each welded to a length of 16 mm mild steel threaded rod, cost me the princely sum of £15, and had I needed the rail itself, no doubt the blacksmith would have knocked this up from a length of 10 x 40 mm mild steel bar. Before installing the brackets, hooks and rails I wire brushed everything and gave it a coat of black Hammerite paint, which I admit is not as good as having all the fittings made from stainless steel, but it runs a close second. Now the whole setup enables me to bring a carcass into the larder, winch it onto

● The hanging rails and wrought iron hooks were salvaged from an old butcher's shop. The suspension brackets were made up by a local blacksmith

a cradle for preparation then up onto the rail for cleaning down and skinning. The only really difficult bit comes when a prepared heavy carcass has to be lifted and manhandled off the hanging rail and into the fridge, but that's the disadvantage of having to work to a limited budget.

Your larder must have adequate lighting. Suspended or surface-mounted fluorescent luminaires suitable for a commercial application will do the job very well, while power points for fridges, winches, freezers and other electrical equipment must also be considered. If situated in a wet area, then appropriate sockets must be specified. Of course all electrical wiring must be carried out by a competent and qualified electrician, and they will be perfectly capable of advising on such matters.

A range of additional equipment and accessories is required for the smooth and efficient operation of the larder. A stainless steel cradle makes the task of removing heads and feet, and opening up the chest cavity if this has not been done in the field, much easier by bringing the carcass to a comfortable working height and holding it steady. It also has the advantage of keeping the carcass off the floor, which of course is beneficial so far as hygiene is concerned.

Good quality knives are essential and if setting up a new establishment it really is worthwhile investing in a set of plastic handled stainless butcher's knives. At the very least a 5- or 6-inch narrow bladed boning knife and a 5 inch broad bladed skinning knife will be necessary, plus a butcher's sharpening steel and a stainless butcher's saw. After use, it is best to clean your knives in the dishwasher as this will have a hot drying mode at the end of its cycle, thus ensuring that your knives are properly sterilised. I would strongly recommend a chain mail glove or at least a Kevlar glove for the hand which is not holding the knife. It is all too easy to slip with a razor-sharp butcher's knife when you are working inside a carcass, possibly

An electric winch makes lifting a large carcass into the lardering cradle an easy task

with numb fingers on a cold winter's evening, and the results of an accident are at best debilitating, at worst very serious indeed and requiring hospital treatment.

A number of spreaders in different lengths to suit different species will be useful, and these can either be bought in stainless steel from a lardering equipment supplier or home-made from high density PTFE water piping. Finally, a good selection of stainless steel gambrels and S hooks is invaluable. I particularly like my two articulated S hooks which enable me to rotate a carcass as I am working on it.

Construction of a properly equipped game larder has made a big difference to my own stalking, enabling me to bring the Land Rover up to the door on my return from the wood, discharge the carcass, prepare it and then take it straight into cold storage with the minimum of fuss. No longer do fallow carcasses have to argue for hanging space with old ropes and garden implements in a dusty old barn, nor do dead muntjac have to frighten the cleaner when she opens the pantry door. And best of all, once they're hung in the chiller, I can skin and butcher deer carcasses at my leisure, rather than having to worry constantly about the ambient temperature and whether my hard-won venison is at risk of deterioration.

14

Dealers and Direct Sales

FOR THE VAST MAJORITY OF STALKERS, the destination of most carcasses will be the AGHE or game dealer. Most dealers have excellent facilities, with many premises having been substantially upgraded since the introduction of the 2006 Regulations. Dealers will usually pay a good price for the larger species, especially red or fallow, which are suitable for the bigger cuts of meat required by the catering industry, though of course that price may well change throughout the season, tracking demand from consumers and the restaurant trade. Before the

● The destination of most carcasses, especially those of the larger species, will be the game dealer

● Customers in this German delicatessen will pay a handsome price for quality roe and red venison

Christmas rush, prices will usually be buoyant; after the New Year's holiday they may well decrease. Roe venison commands a premium, for it is in great demand for export to continental Europe where it is especially highly prized. Indeed, a walk around some of the more exclusive delicatessens during a visit to Berlin opened my eyes to just how keenly the discerning German customer values the best cuts of roe. Muntjac on the other hand is poorly regarded by dealers despite the fact that the flavour and quality of the venison really is quite superb: there is simply not enough of it on a single animal in comparison to the time required to skin and cut the carcass for muntjac to be much of a commercial proposition for the UK market. Having said that, there does now seem to be some interest in the species from customers in Scandinavia.

Naturally, dealers expect a clean and well presented carcass, and of course one which is accompanied by the appropriate hunter declaration which will enable the requisite paperwork to be completed without hitch. Beware: any bullet damage will usually result in deductions from the published price per kilo, because it will require some part of the carcass to be trimmed and discarded as unfit for consumption. This is entirely reasonable. What does annoy me intensely, though, is the tendency for some dealers to pay a premium for animals which have been neck or even head shot. While I can well understand that, from the dealer's point of view, this rewards those who supply carcasses with no blemish to the principal cuts, in my opinion it only encourages risky shooting with consequent implications for deer welfare. I have on occasions had to grit my teeth when delivering a chest shot carcass to the dealer's larder, only to be regaled with stories about how old so-and-so is such a good shot that he always brings in head shot animals. I am sometimes left wondering how many animals there are around old so-and-so's patch with a bottom jaw shot away.

Dealer sales will be considered from the moment a deer is shot, and both the employed estate stalker and the independent amateur shooting on his own ground will be looking to ensure that carcass quality can be maintained as efficiently as possible until the deer is hanging in the dealer's chiller. However, most recreational stalkers will wish to retain at least the occasional carcass to provide venison for their own freezer or perhaps for that of their stalking landlord. Even the sporting estate which disposes of most of its carcasses to the dealer will often require venison for home consumption by the landowner and his guests, and an assessment will therefore be made as to which animals need to be prepared for the dealer's larder and which should be retained. Sometimes this judgement will be made according to how many carcasses there are of what species at the conclusion of a stalking session, while it might also relate to the amount – if any – of damage to

● Carcasses sold to the dealer will be tagged so that they can be traced throughout the food chain

● Many game dealers have invested heavily in upgrading their premises

a carcass resulting from a misplaced shot, the way the animal was standing or simply the way it moved its legs in the split second that the trigger was pulled. Perhaps it is the better quality carcass which will be destined for the dealer, with the damaged ones retained in order that any good venison might be salvaged for home consumption. Or perhaps some stalkers might even prefer to keep the best ones for themselves. If so, then they should expect no favours from the dealer.

The new framework of laws and regulations with which we must now comply does, however, open up yet another alternative, and that is the preparation of game and venison for onward sale. For nearly 150 years this was prohibited to all who did not hold a Game Dealer's Licence, and though some larger estates did in fact hold such licences and deal in game, direct venison sales were by and large unusual. The

● European regulations recognise the close association between the hunter and the quarry that he has killed

● These carcasses are ready for butchering into saleable venison under the hunter exemption

abolition in 2007 of the Game Dealer's Licence* has opened up a range of new opportunities, both for the sporting estate that wishes to add value to its own products through processing and onward sale to customers at, say, a farm shop, and indeed to the independent stalker who is shooting more deer than he requires for his own purposes. Game dealers who have invested heavily in the upgrading of their own premises to AGHE standards may naturally look askance at the emergence of such local direct sales, though in truth they too can benefit, perhaps by processing and packaging venison for direct sale by a local estate, which can thus reap the rewards of selling its own produce but is at the same time freed from the need to invest in food processing premises and skilled labour. Besides which I would contend that anything which serves to stimulate the public demand for quality game and venison is good for the entire industry.

The new European Regulation, however, is very specific in that it recognises the close association between the hunter and the quarry which he himself has hunted, killed and turned into game meat fit for entry into the food chain. The so-called 'hunter exemption' enables the person who shoots alone or who takes an active part in hunting – and is not merely a spectator – to sell game meat, as opposed to unskinned carcasses, without having to develop his premises into an AGHE.

Only game that has been shot by the hunter in question or members of his party may be sold under this exemption, so it would not be permitted, for example, for a deer stalker proposing to sell venison to buy-in carcasses from other estates for processing and re-sale. Furthermore, the regulations provide that only small quantities of game meat may be supplied, either direct to the final consumer or to local retailers that directly supply the final consumer. 'Small quantities' in this context are regarded as self-defining, because demand from final customers and local retailers is limited.

* The Regulatory Reform (Game) Order 2007 abolished the requirement under the Game Licences Act 1860 for those trading in game and venison in England and Wales to hold a Game Dealer's Licence. Similar legislation is, at the time of writing, under consultation in Scotland.

● Under the hunter exemption, a stalker may supply venison to local pubs and restaurants

Thus a stalker may supply the final consumer with venison which he himself or another member of his stalking party has shot and prepared. Such supply is not restricted to local customers, and the stalker may therefore sell over the internet or by mail order if he wishes to do so, as well as selling to those customers visiting his premises or to whom he delivers.

He may also supply local retailers who supply the final consumer, such as pubs, restaurants or retail butchers. 'Local' retailers are defined as those within the county of the stalker's own premises, plus the greater of either the neighbouring county or counties, or 50 km (30 miles) from the boundary of the county of the stalker's premises. Note that 'local' is defined by the regulations with reference to where the stalker has his premises and not to where the venison was shot, so a stalker may shoot deer on a variety of estates, bring them back to his own premises for preparation and sell the venison to local retailers under the hunter exemption.

Stalking estates may also benefit from the hunter exemption and use it to sell their own venison at, say, a farm or estate shop or through local retailers, thereby developing a strong local brand identity amongst consumers in the area. In doing so, however, they must ensure that only those who are directly involved with the hunting of the deer prepare the venison. Thus the estate stalker, gamekeeper or ghillie would be entitled to prepare the meat, but not another estate employee who was unconnected with the stalking party. An estate could not, for example, employ a butcher to process the venison and still continue to operate under the hunter exemption. Nor could it, under the hunter exemption, buy in carcasses from elsewhere and process them into venison for sale at its farm shop. In either case it would instead have to convert its premises into an AGHE. However, a perfectly legitimate alternative for the estate wishing to develop its own local venison brand whilst utilising the services of a professional butcher would be to contract out its processing and packaging to a nearby AGHE. Many game dealers undertake such services for local estates and are delighted to do so.

The hunter exemption introduces a welcome element of freedom into the marketing of game and venison by those involved in producing it. However, it does not absolve a stalker or an estate wishing to sell venison from having to comply with a range of other food and food safety legislation. From the moment the stalker ceases to produce venison solely for himself or as gifts or very occasional sales to his friends and neighbours, and starts selling it commercially to members of the public or to the local pub or restaurant, then he is conducting a food business, and he must register with the Environmental Health Department of his District Council.

Construction standards for food business premises are rather stricter than those for premises such as a larder which is only used to store carcasses in-skin before onward transmission to an AGHE. Their layout and design must permit adequate cleaning and protect against the build-up of dirt, there must be adequate flush lavatories and hand washing facilities, there must be suitable natural or artificial ventilation,

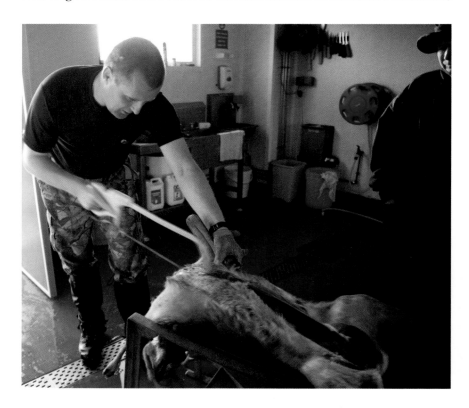

● Food business premises must be constructed to a high standard which ensures hygiene and cleanliness

there must be adequate lighting and drainage, changing facilities for personnel must be provided where necessary and there must be suitable storage for cleaning and disinfectant agents away from areas where food is stored and handled.

Different local authorities will have their own procedures, but in the first instance you should contact your Environmental Health Office, which will ask you to apply for the registration of a food business establishment under Regulation (EC) No 852/2004 on the hygiene of foodstuffs, Article 6(2). You will be required to provide the address of the premises from which you plan to operate plus any trading name for the business, and to indicate the nature of the business which you intend to run. Expect a visit from your local environmental health officer, who will wish to see and inspect your premises – for example the larder where you are storing carcasses and the cutting room in which you are converting them into saleable venison. Your environmental health officer will accept that if you are just starting to trade in a small way, then you may be making use of your own domestic facilities, for example by cutting carcasses on a kitchen table. That should not be a problem, provided that correct hygiene procedures are strictly observed.

You will, however, be expected to put into place a written food safety system which complies with HACCP (Hazard Analysis and Critical Control Points) guidance for those producing wild game meat. This will cover all stages of the preparation process, from the acceptance of carcasses, through skinning and evisceration, chilling, inspection, cutting and trimming, packaging and dispatch. You will also be required under the Environmental Protection Act 1990 to have put in place some suitable procedure for the disposal of trade waste. From the moment that you start selling venison, as opposed to cutting it for your own personal consumption, the skins, bones and other trimmings or appendages such as heads and feet are no longer domestic or kitchen waste but trade waste and must be disposed of accordingly, perhaps by arrangement with a local wholesale butcher.

Direct sale of venison, like marriage, is not to be entered into lightly or wantonly, but advisedly and soberly. It requires a good deal of thought, proper planning and possibly not a little investment in premises, equipment and training. However, if properly undertaken it can offer a valuable new income stream to a sporting estate or enterprise whilst at the same time helping to generate new interest in venison amongst local consumers who perhaps are used to seeing wild deer in the countryside and are interested to know what they taste like.

● Sale of well-presented venison is a very rewarding experience for the deer stalker

It also gives the stalker new respect for a quarry which he can now take from the fields or woods all the way to the consumer.

I remember an Essex farmer once telling me that, as a young man, he quickly realised that he knew nothing about growing potatoes until he had stood beside a barrow in the East End selling to thrifty, critical Londoners the spuds he had produced on his own farm. By the same token, believe me that there is nothing that enables one better to enthuse a potential customer with the delights of cooking and eating venison than having killed, processed and butchered a beast, then carefully and expertly cut it and packaged it for sale. It is also a hugely rewarding experience, with the feedback and comments one receives from customers forming yet another link in the process of turning deer carcasses into quality venison.

15 From Larder to Kitchen

EVERY MONTH OR SO, I receive an email from my local British Deer Society branch secretary informing me of the events and activities which have been arranged by the branch for the benefit of local members. Some are hugely popular, others less so. Occasionally activities are cancelled through lack of support, but one event which was oversubscribed twice over was a butchery demonstration at which deer stalkers were invited to learn from a professional butcher the skills of cutting a deer carcass. Those of us who regularly eat meat that we ourselves have taken from Britain's countryside have always had an interest in how best to convert furred and feathered game into tasty and attractive food on our tables, but I take a particular delight in the number of deer stalkers who are now keen to develop their skills in turning carcasses into professionally presented cuts of meat.

There has in recent years been a huge surge of interest in the production and processing of meat which is either wild, local or both. This reawakening of appreciation by the British public in the fantastic flavour and texture of regional produce and natural foods from the countryside has been driven by some of our more influential TV chefs and has greatly benefited sales of game and venison. Both BASC and the Countryside Alliance have helped the process along the way by providing marketing support, and the Alliance's Game-to-Eat campaign recorded a 64 per cent increase in game sales over the six years after it was launched in 2002.

People are now genuinely much more interested in the food they eat. They want to know where their meat has come from, whether it has been farmed organically and what breed it is. In the case of venison, they at least want to know whether it is farmed or wild, and some consumers are keen to know whether the animal was shot locally. There

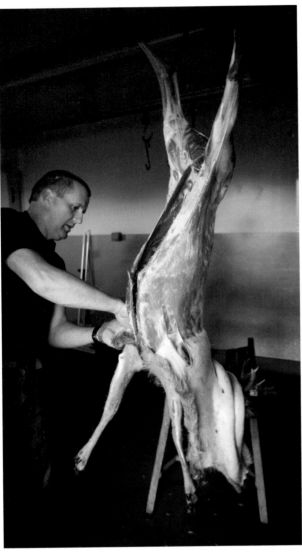

● Skinning a newly killed animal which is still warm is much easier than skinning a cold carcass

is no doubt that wild venison with a guaranteed provenance of the estate on which it is sold, suitably packaged and labelled, has a large and growing market. At present, I don't believe the average British consumer, unlike his or her counterpart in continental Europe, has sufficient knowledge to make a choice between venison of different species, but I think that with appropriate marketing and consumer information, this will come. When it does, there will be the opportunity for venison suppliers to get the best price for top quality meat such as roe haunch and fillet. Furthermore, while it will always be red and, especially, fallow which will supply the bulk of the locally sourced wild venison market in England, I know from experience that a well presented muntjac haunch makes a very saleable family-sized roasting joint. If more consumers were to discover the attraction of muntjac venison for themselves, then it would not be very long before deer stalkers started to find a sensible outlet for their muntjac carcasses, which in turn would give a significant boost to the management of this rather neglected species.

Meanwhile, muntjac and of course roe are the species that tend to be retained and processed for home consumption by the amateur deer stalker while other larger and more saleable carcasses will usually go to the dealer or AGHE. Preparing a carcass really is very easy and with a bit of practice it is possible to achieve a level of presentation which is equal to anything you can find in the butcher's chiller cabinet.

The process starts with skinning, which can be undertaken either at the time the carcass is taken into the larder or alternatively after it has hung in the chiller for a few days. I quickly learned when I helped out at a hunt kennels during my school holidays that skinning a newly killed animal which is still warm is much easier than skinning a cold carcass, and these days I have a preference for skinning deer the moment they arrive home at the larder. The skin pulls away with much less pressure from the hands and requires very little assistance from the knife. When there are just one or two animals involved and the carcasses are not large, skinning does not take very long at all and if it is undertaken as part of the lardering process then this will reduce the washing-down time by at least 50 per cent, for instead of washing down the larder once when the animal is brought in and prepared for the chiller and again a few days later when it has been skinned, only one cleaning operation is required.

Bear in mind that once a skinned carcass is in the chiller, any further animals that are taken in must also be skinned in order to avoid possible cross-contamination. Furthermore, storage of a skinned carcass is likely to result in greater weight loss in the venison than storage of a carcass in the skin. On balance, though, and from the perspective of the amateur stalker, I feel that if there is sufficient time available on your return from stalking, then it is preferable if you have the opportunity to do so, to skin immediately a carcass which you intend to keep.

After hanging it in the chiller, ideally for a few days to allow the meat to 'set', the carcass can be butchered. It is a pretty straightforward process, though one which gets easier with practice, and if you have experience of preparing rabbits or hares for the kitchen then you will find that the basic anatomy of a deer is not dissimilar, just bigger. Sometimes a lot bigger.

Lay the carcass on a spacious, washable surface such as melamine or stainless steel. Being more of a traditionalist, I use a large marble slab. Removing the forequarters is easy, because these are attached only by muscles and membranes which can be cut through with ease as the foreleg is pushed gently away from the chest. Tracing around the outside edge of the shoulder blade with a sharp filleting knife will allow the foreleg to come away from the chest in its entirety.

The haunches may be removed by severing the spinal column at the front end of the pelvis and then using a butcher's saw to cut along the median line of the pelvis, thus dividing the two haunches. Alternatively, and this is the procedure which I invariably use, bone the two haunches in turn away from the pelvic girdle. Taking a filleting knife, make a cut to the underside of the pelvis down the median line, score with the knife around the pelvic bone and back along the spine, then fillet the muscle away from the bone, detaching the hip joint as you do so. Eventually the entire haunch will come away from the bone leaving virtually no waste at all and producing an excellent joint, either for roasting or for further processing.

● The illustrations show the preparation of a muntjac, but the same procedures may be used for larger species

1 Cut through the muscle and membrane of the forequarters

2 Trace around the outside of the shoulder blade to remove the foreleg

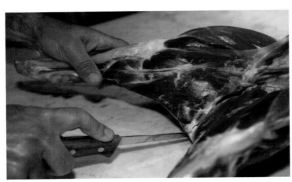

3 To bone out the haunches, make a cut to the underside of the pelvis down the median line

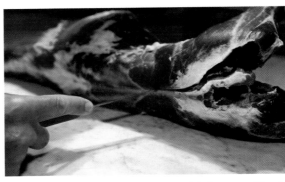

4 Score with the knife around the pelvic bone and back along the spine

5 Fillet the muscle away from the bone, detaching the hip joint

6 Make a cut to the front of the pelvic bone

7 Detach the haunch

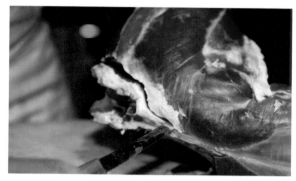

8 Repeat the process for the other haunch

9 Fillet the second haunch away from the bone

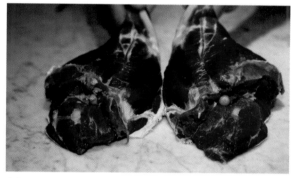

10 Both haunches are now detached

11 To produce a neater joint, saw through the shank bone just below the knuckle

12 Both haunches are ready for packaging

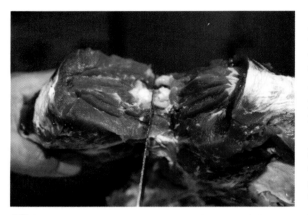

13 Detach the neck by making a cut forward of the front ribs, then twisting and breaking the spine

Having repeated the process for the second haunch, I detach the neck by making a cut forward of the front ribs right up to the spine, continuing that cut around the top of the spine and then twisting and breaking the spine at that point. If you have made your cuts correctly, the neck will come away very easily.

My usual procedure thereafter is to remove the fillets, also known as the loin strips. Make a deep cut as close as possible to the spine, following the spine all the way from the neck to the pelvis. Work the filleting knife underneath the fillets, stroking it gently across the rib cage and drawing the fillets down and away as you do so, finally

14 To remove the fillets, make a deep cut close to the spine

15 Work the filleting knife underneath the fillets

16 Draw the fillets down and away

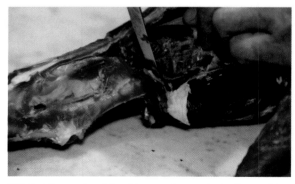

17 Cut the ends of the fillets underneath the front of the pelvic bone

18 Pull the fillets away from the rib cage, separating them from the hard membrane

detaching them with an angled cut under the front of the pelvis. As you pull the fillets away from the rib cage, separate them from as much of the hard membrane as will easily come away without damaging them. The top side of each fillet is covered with a silvery skin, which may be removed later with the filleting knife.

An alternative method of butchering is to leave the loins on the bone and to remove the bone-in saddle, cutting the spine with the saw immediately in front of the pelvis and between the fourth and fifth rib, counting from the back of the rib cage. Then, using first the knife and then the saw, trim the ends of the ribs along the line of the lower edge of the loin or fillet muscle. It's a bit more work, but it makes a nice roasting joint if that's what you like, especially on a larger carcass like a fallow. Personally, I think that the fillets are too good for roasting on the bone.

Finally, turning the carcass over, carefully remove the tenderloins, also known as fillets or undercuts, with the filleting knife. You have then removed all the principal cuts and joints. Now it is time to strip the carcass. Do this by trimming away the flank muscle – the abdominal

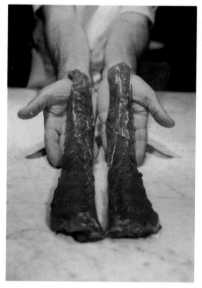

19 Both fillets are ready for packaging

20 Turning the carcass over, carefully remove the tenderloins

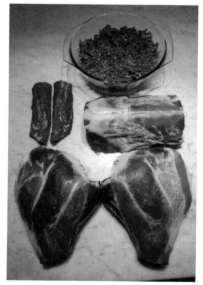

21 An alternative method of preparation, leaving the saddle intact as a roasting joint

22 Trimming away the flank muscle and the rib flank

wall – and the rib flank, taking care to cut away and separate out all shot-damaged meat. If the carcass is one of the larger species, then it is profitable, having removed the rib flank, to cut the meat from between the ribs themselves. This leaves the rib cage and spinal column totally stripped of meat.

By now I have built up a series of piles on my work surface. These are the main joints, namely the haunches and forequarters; two fillet or loin strips; the neck; and two piles of trimmings, one comprising good quality meat and the other comprising anything which is bruised, blackened, shot damaged, soiled or contaminated in any way. Now it is time to decide how to deal with all those piles.

If the animal is of a smaller species, such as a roe or muntjac, I usually keep the haunches whole for roasting, simply trimming off the shank or lower part of the leg with the saw to make a neater package for the freezer or roasting tin. In the case of a larger species, the haunch will usually be far too large to roast as a single joint, though if there is a forthcoming grand event such as a large Christmas meal or, in one case, a dinner for sixteen at a Scottish shooting lodge, then a fallow haunch might be consigned to the freezer in its entirety and marked accordingly. More usually, I separate out the individual muscles from the haunch, carefully dividing them and paring them away from the bone. The resulting haunch steak is meat of the finest quality, suitable for grilling, frying or cooking on the barbecue, and I pack it in meal-sized portions.

The very best meat is that on the two fillets or loin strips. This really is melt-in-mouth stuff and to my mind there is no finer venison than the fillet of a young roe or a muntjac. It is tender, fine grained, succulent, and to be treated with reverence. If you are processing venison for sale under the 'hunter exemption' then this is the bit which you retain for your own consumption. In my household, muntjac fillet is regarded as the ultimate fast food, to be rolled lightly in sea salt and crushed peppercorns and then seared in the top oven of the Aga for eleven minutes before it is sliced into tender, moist, pink noisettes and served with a few home grown vegetables or, more prosaically, oven chips and frozen peas. However, the fillets must be prepared before use by removing the silver membrane which covers the upper side of the muscle and if you do not intend to eat the fillets immediately then it is well worth doing this job before putting them into the freezer.

23 Bone out the forequarter meat

24 A good quality electric mincer really is a good investment

Meat from the forequarters is of lesser quality. The muscles on the forelegs are not so large and furthermore, the forelegs are the edible parts of the carcass which are most susceptible to bullet damage should the animal not have been standing exactly square-on to the shooter when the shot was fired. Because of this I usually strip all the meat off the forequarters, putting that from the shoulder with the better quality offcuts and that from the lower leg into the lower grade pile, along with the flank. The shoulder meat, plus any other quality offcuts, can be diced and is perfect for casseroles and stews. Necks, too can be reserved for stews after they have been suitably trimmed to remove all damaged, bloodied or bruised meat.

All shot-damaged or otherwise rejected trimmings I place in a casserole and cook up for the dogs, who are always delighted with the result. If a big batch of venison is being prepared, then dog food gets put into plastic ice cream tubs and frozen for future use.

The best way to prepare trimmings from the flanks and lower legs is as mince. Minced venison is perfect for Bolognese sauces or chilli; it makes a fantastic 'stalker's pie', which is the venison equivalent of shepherd's pie, and it can be used instead of minced beef in virtually any other recipe. There's only one problem: you need a mincer. If you are preparing any substantial number of carcasses in the course of a year, then a good quality electric mincer really is a good investment, for it will more than pay for itself in the savings you make from your ability to convert low grade carcass trimmings into excellent minced venison. A good domestic mincer can be obtained for under £150, but if you are expecting to make a lot of mince, then a professional quality machine starts at around £250. Quality mince is also the foundation for sausage making, as I shall describe shortly.

Do not neglect the bones or consign them immediately to a black plastic bin bag, for they form the basic ingredient of the most exquisite stock. A large casserole is required, and the best bones to use are the long bones from the legs, which should be split or broken with a meat cleaver to allow the marrow to be rendered out. However, all freshly stripped venison bones will make excellent stock. Cover the bones with cold water and add a peeled and quartered onion and a few sprigs of fresh herbs such as rosemary, sage or thyme. Then bring the casserole to the boil and place in a very slow oven overnight. In the morning, drain the stock into containers suitable for the freezer. Another trick is to put it into 250 ml yoghurt pots and freeze these. When frozen, the blocks of stock can be removed from the pots and bundled together in a single bag, enabling the cook to select a neat little recipe-sized chunk of delicious stock for cooking with. Venison stock made in this way is the perfect base for game soups and will add another dimension to casseroles or braised meat of any sort.

1 Place the meat in a vacuum pouch and insert the open end into the machine

2 When the air is extracted, the heat seal strip is activated to weld the end of the pouch

3 Minced venison can be packed in polystyrene trays

4 Venison prepared and packed for freezing

Although a certain amount of venison may well be refrigerated and consumed within a few hours of processing, the majority will almost certainly be consigned to the deep freezer. However, when packed in conventional polythene freezer bags, venison still has a limited life in a freezer. If all the air is not removed from the package, then food will change colour through oxidation, and flavour and nutrients are lost. In any case, conventional one-ply bags will deteriorate during storage and eventually allow air to permeate through microscopic cracks and fissures. Most of us who keep a well-stocked deep freezer have seen and tasted the unpleasant effect of 'freezer burn' on our hard-won supplies of game meat.

Vacuum packing changes all that. By placing a joint of meat in a high-density vacuum pouch, removing the air from the pack with a vacuum pump and sealing it, storage life is trebled. Instead of lasting just six months in your freezer, venison will remain fresh for eighteen months. Furthermore, when vacuum packed the meat sits flatter, takes up less freezer space and is far easier to mark or label. Not only that, the packages look far more professional too.

A home vacuum packer is extremely easy to operate. Just place the meat into a suitably sized vacuum pouch, insert the open end into the machine and push the 'start' button. The vacuum pump whirrs into action and if you have an automatic machine, when all the air is extracted, the pump stops and the heat seal strip is activated to weld the end of the pouch. The whole process takes just a few seconds. If you add an expanded polystyrene tray into the equation and seal your mince, steaks and fillets in neat 450 gram packs, the presentation is as good as anything your local butcher can produce.

Smoking a joint

Frequent stalkers who regularly bring substantial numbers of carcasses home for domestic preparation and consumption by family and friends, though they may never tire of the prime cuts, will eventually start to look for alternative ways of preparing venison.

Smoking is one of the oldest methods of preserving food, but it is so shrouded in mystique that the average connoisseur of fine food has been reluctant to try out the process, either because he or she believes that lots of complicated infrastructure is involved or for fear of mucking up expensive ingredients, or both.

Years ago I experimented with smoking fish, which I hung from a hook inside a large brick chimney above the open fire in our cottage. It

● *Above left:* A Char Broil H$_2$O hot smoker

● *Above right:* Cover the hot charcoal with fragments of wood which have previously been soaked in water

was not a success. More recently I bought a commercially made smoker which looks like a large green metal dustbin, and started hot smoking venison. The smoker actually comprises two principal chambers: a lower section which provides the heat source and an upper chamber which takes the food plus a large enamel bowl of hot water. This is topped off by a lid with a wooden handle and a temperature gauge.

To operate the smoker, you build a charcoal fire in the lower section and when the charcoal is white, at the stage at which you would put the

● *Right:* Place your venison on the grill trays

● *Above left:* Be patient and let the smoker do its work

● *Above right:* There is nothing nicer for a summer's picnic than a smoked muntjac haunch carved off the bone

sausages on if you were barbecuing, you cover it with fragments and splinters of wood which have been previously soaked for a couple of hours in a bucket of water. I use oak from one of the woods where I stalk, which seems to me particularly appropriate. However, fruit wood, maple and many other hardwoods are equally suitable. There is no need to use sawdust, such as one might use in some of the cold smokers that my angling friends possess. Just a log of oak split into little bits with a hand axe is all that is required.

At the same time as you start generating smoke, you must place two kettles full of boiling water in the water pan which sits immediately above the fire. This means that the food chamber is filled not merely with smoke but with steam, thereby ensuring that the food remains moist during the cooking process and does not dry out. An onion and some sprigs of herb such as rosemary or sage in the water will help to impart extra flavour into the steam.

Over the hot water pan, within the food chamber, are two grill trays on which you place the food to be smoked. The recipe books say that the food should be brined before smoking, but I have never found this necessary. Brining ensures the food is moist before cooking commences, but exactly the same moistness can be achieved by taking a joint out of the freezer and defrosting it.

The thermometer which is built in to the top of the smoker provides some guidance to the internal temperature, but thereafter calculating the cooking time is seat-of-the-pants stuff. In the summer, when ambient temperatures are high, you can cook things a lot more quickly than on a frosty January day. I hot smoked one load of venison inside two hours on one blazing August day, but that's unusual. Three to four hours usually seems to be about right, but do not on any account open the inspection door once cooking has commenced. If you do, then oxygen will be introduced to the fire and the whole lot will ignite in a mass of flame. Just be patient, wait for the requisite period and then remove the food once it is cooked.

Like many keen field sports enthusiasts, my wife and I have freezer loads of game and venison in the larder, and smoking was at first an experimental attempt to do something different with the seemingly endless quantities of fallow, muntjac, pheasant, duck and goose which were generated each winter. I was really not prepared for the way that smoking transformed a staple food like venison into something utterly delectable, into a meat with the subtle smoky flavour of the forest and a tenderness that made it almost fall from the bone.

Our regular fare is the muntjac haunch, and a couple of muntjac haunches plus three or four pheasants make a perfect load for the smoker. The birds or beasts can be eaten hot from the smoker or cold. There is absolutely nothing nicer for a summer's picnic lunch with friends than a smoked muntjac haunch carved off the bone in gorgeous, soft, pink slivers. Naturally the outer skin of the meat is fairly hard and brown in colour after exposure to the heat and smoke, so I carefully pare this away to get to the succulent stuff inside. However, there is nothing in the rules to say that, having smoked a joint, you cannot then re-freeze it. We do, and we have found that when properly packed, smoked venison freezes extremely well. Smoking is quite a lot of work, rather fiddly and of course you can't do it indoors, but otherwise there isn't really a downside.

Sausages

A further exploration into the world of meat processing has involved the quest for the perfect venison sausage. Like food smoking, sausage production is a step too far for the average cook, but the availability of endless supplies of low grade venison offcuts slowly but surely sets the more adventurous gastronomically inclined deer stalker thinking about the endless possibilities which are presented by the humble sausage.

Sausage making is not difficult, but a certain amount of specialist equipment and materials are needed and there is a decided knack involved. The starting point is the mince which I referred to when I discussed the essentials of venison preparation, but sausages will require something more than undiluted lean venison mince if they are to be moist and flavoursome. The recipe books suggest an admixture of minced fat pork belly in order to raise the overall fat content of the mixture. This certainly works very well, but so does venison suet, stripped from around the kidneys and the lining of the abdominal cavity. My wife and I once made a batch of roe sausages using solely minced roe trimmings plus suet taken from a couple of very fat end-of-season does. They were absolutely delicious.

A further addition to the sausage mix is rusk, which comes ready prepared in fine crumbs and is available from a commercial supplier of sausage making paraphernalia in large bags. Not very much is needed, and a 1 kg (2½ lb) bag of rusk will be enough for around 20 lbs of sausages. To the basic mince, fat and rusk mixture, you must then add your seasonings, and it is these which will determine the final flavour of your sausages. Do not stint on the seasoning. When making our first batch of sausages we followed a recipe which seemed to call for so much salt and pepper that we simply couldn't believe that it was correct. But we were wrong and the recipe was right. A good basic mix seems to be:

> 2½ lb venison
> 8 oz pork fat or venison suet
> 1 cup rusk crumbs
> 1 tablespoon sea salt
> 1 teaspoon freshly ground black pepper

Thereafter add whatever flavouring ingredient you wish. We always feel that juniper berries have a particular affinity for venison, since they impart the fresh taste of the Scottish hill – or the Scandinavian forests, which is where I more frequently pick them. Rosemary has a similar quality, though it is available much closer to the kitchen, while sage is a traditional sausage making ingredient. A slug of alcohol makes a particularly attractive addition to the mix, and I have made some quite amazing sausages with the simple addition of a large glug of Islay single malt whisky.

● Making venison sausages

● *Above left:* Mix the ingredients together

● *Above right:* Add a glass of wine, or possibly something stronger

Once you are happy with your mixture, the fun begins. It is possible to make sausages with a hand-operated sausage stuffer, but it is so much easier and quicker with an electric mincer, fitted with a sausage stuffing nozzle. This is a long, cone-shaped gadget which allows you to direct the flow of sausage mixture straight into the casing, or sausage skin. Casings may be obtained from a specialist supplier. Artificial casing is perfectly acceptable, but far better is natural casing which is easier to use and less liable to burst or tear. Unlike artificial casing, which is dried, natural casing has a limited shelf life although it keeps very well in the freezer. All casing must be well soaked before use, to make it soft and pliable, and after soaking it must be pushed over the stuffing nozzle. The addition of a few drops of olive oil smeared over the stuffing nozzle and inside the casing will make this rather tricky task a lot easier. With your casing in place and your mincer tray charged with sausage mixture, switch on the mincer and draw the

● Draw the casing off
the nozzle as the mixture
is extruded into it

casing off the nozzle as the mixture is extruded into it. This really is a job for two, one operating the mincer while the other manipulates the casing.

Do not over-fill the casing, otherwise it will burst either as you extrude the sausage or later when you try to form the individual links.

● *Above left:* The prepared sausage and (left) sausages twisted into links ready for freezing or cooking

● *Above right:* The final result: delicious home-made venison sausages

A few trial runs will soon guide you towards the right amount of mixture to insert and before you know it, sausage making will be both easy, fun, and the source of endless experimentation with new flavourings.

Remember that sausages made for home consumption without any preservative have an extremely short shelf life. When you have made them into links, they must either be refrigerated for use within the next couple of days or frozen for longer term storage. We find that half a dozen sausages fit neatly into a small re-sealable plastic tray that stores well in the freezer and enables us to draw off just three or four sausages whenever we need them without the need to defrost an entire pack. For believe me, though they may look deceptively small, these sausages are truly man-sized. Just a couple of them, braised slowly in shredded onions and venison stock, and served with creamy mashed home-grown potatoes, is the sort of bangers-and-mash for which you would pay a king's ransom at a smart gastro-pub, if you were ever lucky enough to find it on the menu.

Finally, do remember to clean your mincer and sausage making gear thoroughly and immediately after use. Some items such as cutting dies and metal castings may well be dishwasher proof, in which case a cycle through the dishwasher will render them clean and sterile. Otherwise spend the requisite amount of time at the kitchen sink with a washing-up brush and plenty of hot water.

Appendix

Close Seasons for Deer

ENGLAND & WALES

Species	Sex	Close season
Red	male	1 May – 31 July
Red	female	1 April – 31 October
Fallow	male	1 May – 31 July
Fallow	female	1 April – 31 October
Sika	male	1 May – 31 July
Sika	female	1 April – 31 October
Roe	male	1 November – 31 March
Roe	female	1 April – 31 October
Chinese water deer	male	1 April – 31 October
Chinese water deer	female	1 April – 31 October
Red/sika hybrids	male	1 May – 31 July
Red/sika hybrids	female	1 April – 31 October

All dates shown are inclusive. There is no statutory close season for muntjac.

SCOTLAND

Species	Sex	Close season
Red	male	21 October – 30 June
Red	female	16 February – 20 October
Fallow	male	1 May – 31 July
Fallow	female	16 February – 20 October
Sika	male	21 October – 30 June
Sika	female	16 February – 20 October
Roe	male	21 October – 31 March
Roe	female	1 April – 20 October
Red/sika hybrids	male	21 October – 30 June
Red/sika hybrids	female	16 February – 20 October

Useful Contacts

British Association for Shooting and Conservation
Marford Mill
Rossett
Wrexham   LL12 0HL
Tel: 01244 573000
Email: enquiries@basc.org.uk
Internet: www.basc.org.uk

British Deer Society
The Walled Garden
Burgate Manor
Fordingbridge
Hampshire   SP6 1EF
Tel: 01425 655434
Email: h.q@bds.org.uk
Internet: www.bds.org.uk

Countryside Alliance
367 Kennington Road
London   SE11 4PT
Tel: 020 7840 9200
Email: info@countryside-alliance.org
Internet: www.countryside-alliance.org

Deer Initiative
The Carriage House
Brynkinalt Business Centre
Chirk
Wrexham   LL14 5NS
Tel: 0845 872 4956
Email: info@thedeerinitiative.co.uk
Internet: www.thedeerinitiative.co.uk

Federation of Field Sports Associations of the EU (FACE)
Rue F Pelletier 82
B-1030 Brussels
Belgium
Tel: 00322 7326 900
Email: info@face.eu
Internet: www.face.eu

Game and Wildlife Conservation Trust
Burgate Manor
Fordingbridge
Hampshire   SP6 1EF
Tel: 01425 652381
Email: info@gwct.org.uk
Internet: www.gwct.org.uk

Scottish Natural Heritage Wildlife Operations Unit
Great Glen House
Leachkin Road
Inverness   IV3 8NW
Tel: 01463 725000
Email: enquiries@snh.gov.uk
Internet: www.snh.gov.uk

Index